J.A. Shuffrey
1859 – 1939

An Oxford Artist's
Life Remembered

by
Lauren Gilmour
and
Margaret Shuffrey

Rural Publications

First published in the United Kingdom in 2003 by
Rural Publications, Print-Rite, 31 Parklands, Freeland, Witney, Oxon OX29 8HX.
Contact telephone and fax 01993 881662

ISBN 0-9544858-0-7

Typeset in 10/11pt Garamond
Typesetting, design by Karen Robertson
Printed in Great Britain by
Artisan Ltd, Kingston Bagpuize, Oxford.

James Allen Shuffrey

by Margaret Shuffrey

Plate 1. James Allen Shuffrey. Portrait by Leslie Banks. Private collection.

James Allen Shuffrey was born in Woodgreen, Witney in Oxfordshire, in 1859. His family were originally blanket weavers but later became tanners and curriers of leather. He moved to Oxford with his wife and children in 1902 and lived there for the rest of his life.

He was a watercolour artist renowned and respected for preserving the memory of the old historical buildings of Oxford through his painting and sketches. He was elected one of the first members of the British Watercolour Society and became well known for his large paintings of the colleges and of the interior of the Cathedral.

From the turn of the century until the 1930s great changes were taking place in Oxford. When he heard of a street or an ancient building which was about to be altered or demolished he would go with his paints and easel to record it before it vanished forever.

He travelled all over Oxfordshire, often on a tricycle, painting the countryside and villages. His travels also took him to Berkshire and Buckinghamshire and each year of his long life he went on a painting tour to a different part of the country.

He visited Antwerp and Bruges in Belgium and was sketching in Bacharach in Germany when war was declared in 1914. He managed to escape internment and arrived home with all his sketches intact.

His fascination with the architecture and the time-softened stone of the colleges and Cathedral never waned. He was still painting at the age of seventy-seven and died in July 1939 at the age of eighty, leaving behind a unique historical record of a much loved, but long vanished Oxford.

Preface

In 1934 Oxford artist James Allen Shuffrey presented fifty of his watercolour paintings and pencil drawings of buildings and scenes in and around the city to the Mayor and people of Oxford. By this act of gratitude, after a commercially successful career in the city spanning three decades, a substantial collection was created, documenting the appearance of Oxford streets, buildings and suburban landscapes from about the 1900s to about the 1930s, reflecting the artist's particular interest in pre 19th century buildings, many of which were soon to disappear in the course of redevelopment. The collection, housed at first in the city's Local Studies Library, was not initially displayed or published, and the artist fell out of public memory except as the designer of several series of Oxford postcards published soon after his arrival there in the early years of the 20th century.

Springing from an artistic family, his creative talents were passed in turn to his son (Reginald), a commercial artist and official First World War artist, and his grandson Tony, a photographer. Tony's wife Margaret, a gifted curator, was inspired to preserve and enlarge a collection of the artist's pictures relating to his early career in Oxfordshire and Sussex during the 1880s and 1890s, and to his excursions by motor bus into the Oxfordshire countryside during the 1920s. These efforts resulted in two private publications in 1987.

In 1974 the group of Oxford pictures passed to Oxfordshire County Council with other Local Studies material. In 1989 these collections were joined to those of the County Museum Service, and the first of two major exhibitions of Shuffrey's work was held at the Museum of Oxford. The 1989 exhibition brought the pictures back into the public arena, displaying a large part of the collection. This proved popular, and a second exhibition was held in 1993, when the opportunity was taken to include material in private hands, notably photographs, Oxfordshire pictures, and some outstanding works from the artist's early years in Oxford. The second exhibition also provided an opportunity to explore the prodigious documentary side of the artist's output, including ledgers, exhibition lists, carefully archived reviews, diaries and memoires, as well as the well-documented family background material.

It was apparent that an exceptional body of information existed about this artist's life, career and artistic methods, setting into context and illuminating the large group of surviving pictures which themselves are so informative about the city and county, and the development of Oxford topographical art, between 1880 and 1930. A determination arose to publish as much of the county's holdings as possible with a full account of the artist's life, work, and social and artistic milieu.

The account begins in Witney in West Oxfordshire, and moves to Abingdon and Sussex before returning to Oxfordshire, but the central theme is that of the topographical artist's presentation of Oxford – timeless, but always hinting at the imminence of change.

Acknowledgments

Thanks must be recorded first and foremost to A.L. Shuffrey FRPS and to Margaret Shuffrey, for consolidating, making accessible and sharing their collection of the artist's pictures, photographs and records; for the huge amount of detailed work that went into the two private publications which formed a starting point for the present publication; for encouraging the County Museum Service to mark the 50th anniversary of Shuffrey's gift to the public with the first exhibition at the Museum of Oxford; for loans and assistance with the second exhibition; and especially for both encouragement and participation in the work of this publication.

The present book could not have been contemplated without the support of Oxfordshire County Council, especially County Museums Officer Martyn Brown, and Nancy Hood, Curator of the Museum of Oxford at the time of the first Shuffrey exhibition. The publications of the Victoria County History office made possible – and vastly enjoyable – the task of researching the locations of the pictures.

Special thanks are due to Dr Malcolm Graham, Head of Oxfordshire Studies; Colin Harrison, Curator of British Art, Department of Western Art, Ashmolean Museum; Julian Munby FSA, Principal Archaeologist, Oxford Archaeology; John Ashdown, formerly Oxford Conservation Officer; Dr Martin Henig, Lecturer at the Institute of Archaeology, University of Oxford and Chair of the Friends of Archives, Museums and Oxfordshire Studies; and Dr Patrick Frazer for taking the time to read the text and make many invaluable corrections and suggestions, although errors and omissions are of course the principal author's own; and to Joan Brasnett for the photography of the Oxford and Oxfordshire collections and A.L. Shuffrey for the photography of the Shuffrey family archive. Particular thanks should be recorded to present and former colleagues at the Museum of Oxford for their support and confidence in both the collection and the authors, and special gratitude to the publisher, Colin Judge. We thank the Bodleian Library, Oxford, for permission to publish the drawings reproduced in *Plates 12, 13, 14 and 15*, and the Ashmolean Museum, Oxford for permission to reproduce *Plates 8 and 117*.

Shuffrey's *Reminiscences*

At the age of seventy-five, Oxford watercolour artist James Allen Shuffrey wrote an account of his long life and artistic career, which had spanned the late Victorian and Edwardian periods and the First World War and its aftermath. Much of it had been spent in and around Oxford. He tackled this project with enthusiasm and clarity. The result is a meticulously handwritten note-book with a narrative running to about 20,000 words, signed and dated 1934, and entitled *Reminiscences (Plate 2)*.

The *Reminiscences*, transcribed by Margaret Shuffrey, wife of the artist's grandson, reveal a modest, good-humoured, and exceptionally independent and well-organised man who from an early age was sensitive to the character of places as well as to the nature of the epoch in which he found himself. An extrovert in social situations, he possessed the ability to observe the local scene with care and attention to detail in the midst of an active daily life devoted to work, family and community affairs. He was especially observant of change, a theme running through the *Reminiscences* and particularly notable in those parts of his account dealing with his Witney childhood and the impact of the First World War on Oxford.

The *Reminiscences* are both a personal account and a document of 19th century social history. As social history, the *Reminiscences* illustrate many of the significant trends that characterised Victorian times. An outstanding feature was the unprecedented growth in population in the UK from about 16 million in 1801 to over 41 million in 1901; between 1841 and 1855 the birth rate remained stable but the death rate declined, so that the population increased by about two million between 1851 and 1891 (Norman McCord, *British History 1815-1906*, Oxford University Press 1991, 76, 212, 315). We learn from

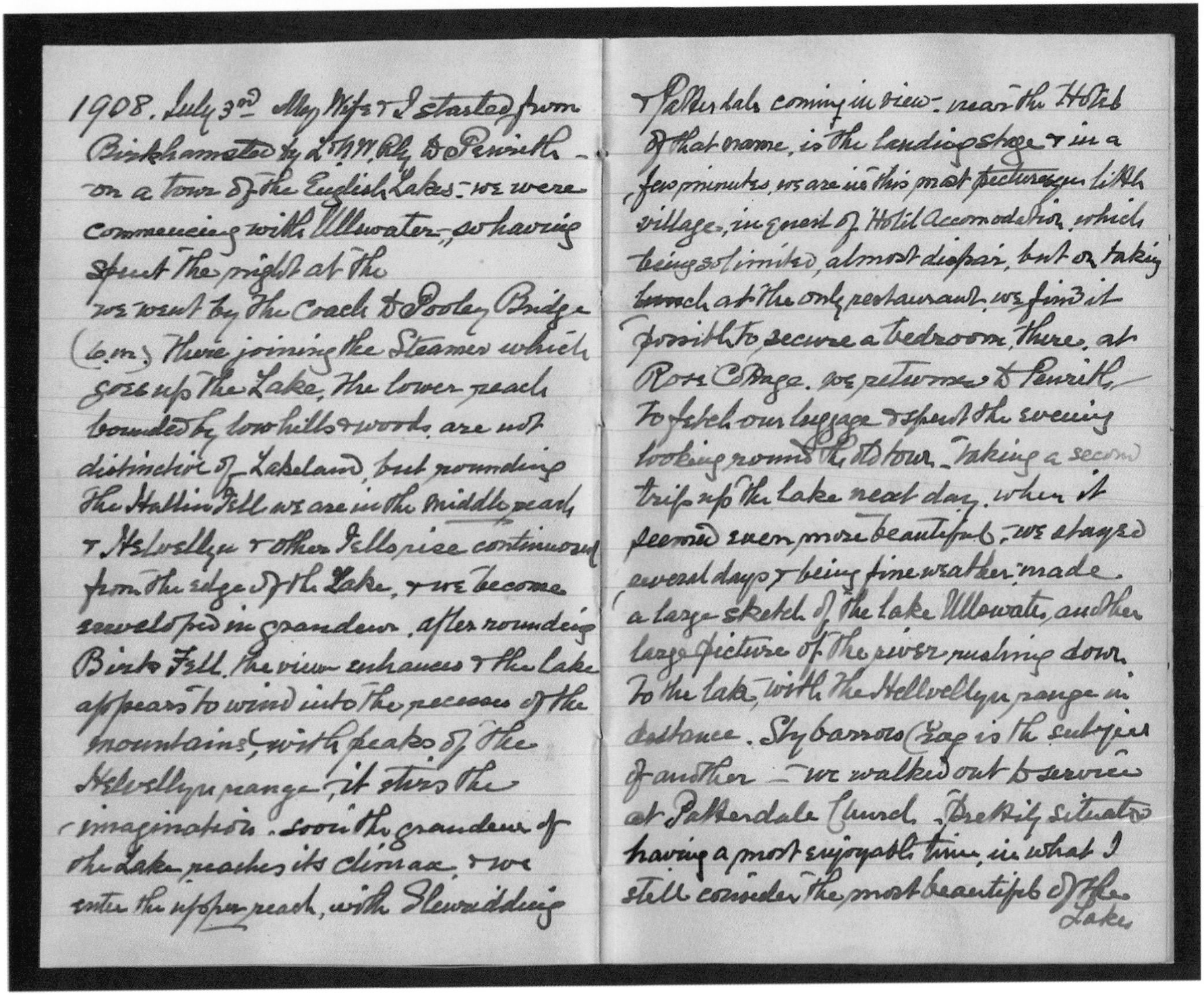

1908. July 3rd My Wife & I started from Birkhamsted by L.N.W. Rly to Penrith - on a tour of the English Lakes - we were commencing with Ullswater, so having spent the night at the [ ] we went by the Coach to Pooley Bridge (6.m) there joining the Steamer which goes up the Lake, the lower reach bounded by low hills & woods, are not distinctive of Lakeland, but rounding the Hallin Fell we are in the middle reach & Helvellyn & other fells rise continuously from the edge of the Lake, & we become enveloped in grandeur. after rounding Birks Fell, the view enhances & the lake appears to wind into the recesses of the mountains, with peaks of the Helvellyn range, it stirs the imagination. soon the grandeur of the Lake reaches its climax, & we enter the upper reach, with Glenridding

& Patterdale coming in view - near the Hotel of that name, is the landing stage & in a few minutes we are in this most picturesque little village, in quest of Hotel Accomodation which being so limited, almost despair, but on taking lunch at the only restaurant, we find it possible to secure a bedroom there, at Rose Cottage. we returned to Penrith, to fetch our luggage & spent the evening looking round the old town. Taking a second trip up the lake next day, when it seemed even more beautiful. we stayed several days & being fine weather, made a large sketch of the lake Ullswater, and other large picture of the river rushing down to the lake, with the Helvellyn range in distance. Stybarrow Crag is the subject of another - we walked out to service at Patterdale Church. Prettily situated having a most enjoyable time, in what I still consider the most beautiful of the Lakes

Plate 2. The first two pages of Shuffrey's *Reminiscences*, written in Oxford in 1934.

the *Reminiscences* that Shuffrey was one of six children who all survived to adulthood, and most produced families of their own. Textile working, although still as important to the national economy in the 19th century as it had been in the 18th, was rapidly changing in character and becoming focussed upon cotton, upon mechanised mills and upon the north-east, to the detriment of woollen weaving and handiwork on a local level (McCord, 216-17). Like thousands of other former woollen weavers the Shuffreys sought new occupations, older sons falling back upon farming in combination with other related lines of work (McCord, 84, 214).

During the middle years of the 19th century schooling became increasingly available, normally in the form of privately run establishments for families able to afford them, like the two schools attended by Shuffrey. Big changes were set in train by the Elementary Education Act of 1870 which established School Boards, systematic training and the setting of standards (McCord, 289-90, 348). The Act was the background to the Cambridge Local Board qualification gained by Shuffrey in 1872, and it is interesting to learn that the London and County Bank was prepared to increase its remuneration to Shuffrey on account of it. The development of recognised professions was another 19th century trend, as a more complex society created a growing need for specialists (McCord, 228, 337). One family member worked as an architect and another as a librarian. Shuffrey narrowly missed the chance of joining a London firm of architects. But as a result of another salient trend of the 19th century, the development of banking and accountancy (McCord, 306-7), he found a respectable occupation for the duration of the 19th century, by which time he had gained the confidence to assume his new identity as a professional artist.

The *Reminiscences* also give us a glimpse of the political attitudes of a young man growing up in West Oxfordshire in the second half of the 19th century. The principal public events that stood out for him were the wedding day of the Prince of Wales, later Edward VII, in 1863; the 1881 Great Volunteer Review before Queen Victoria in Windsor Park, in which he took part; and the relief of Mafeking, a besieged British outpost, during the Boer War, in 1900. As a banker and former farmer the harvest failures and bankruptcies of the 1870s would have concerned him professionally. His membership of the Temperance Society from the 1880s and the Primrose League from 1906 identify him as a pragmatic Conservative concerned about the balance of trade at the national level, and committed to local social activities in support of his beliefs.

From the later 19th century the *Reminiscences* are increasingly concerned with the development of Shuffrey's art and career. From 1877 he had kept a diary of his painting expeditions, undoubtedly a useful aide-memoire when he came to write the *Reminiscences*. He also kept detailed notes of his pictures offered for sale at the Oxford studio and at periodic exhibitions in Oxford, noting in the *Reminiscences* with customary good humour and detachment that one or two pictures of which he was fond had failed to find a purchaser.

The lists and ledgers remind us that from his late 30s following retirement on a small pension from a banking position, he and his family were successfully dependant for their additional income upon his painting – an achievement for any artist.

Background and Influences

James Allen Shuffrey was born in Witney's Woodgreen, his family's home since 1713 when John Shuffrey, his great-great-great-grandfather, a

Plate 4. 7 Narrow Hill, Witney, the Shuffrey family home until 1992.

Plate 3. James' ancestor Samuel Shuffrey, born 1769. A Witney weaver, he converted the old weaving workshops at Wood Green into a factory for currying leather for the shoe trade.

Plate 5. The boys at Mr Collier's school near the Corn Exchange, Witney, in the 1860s. James is fourth from the right in the back row, and his brother Frank third from the right in the middle row.

Plate 6. Samuel Shuffrey, James' father, a Witney tanner, currier and farmer, born 1810.

Huguenot immigrant and a weaver, had settled there and erected weaving workshops at the back of a house at the top of Narrow Hill *(Plate 4)*. Five generations of Shuffreys lived in Woodgreen and engaged in weaving, tanning and currying leather for the Witney shoe trade, and later, farming. The rich arable and pastoral hinterland of Witney on the edge of the Thames Valley and the Oxfordshire Cotswolds, provided temporary work for the sons of the family to help out on the larger farms, like the one at Cogges (where the photographs *Plates 31, 32 and 33* were probably taken) and to engage in gardening and poultry keeping for the busy town's market. As the third son in a family of six children, this is the work for which he would have been destined had not the unexpected opportunity of a banking career intervened.

His early recollections, apart from the ones concerning his school days, are those of a childhood spent largely out-of-doors – in the summer, swimming and fishing for crayfish in the Windrush, cricket, playing with hoops and marbles, catching birds, outdoor fairs, athletics and celebrations; in the winter, ice-skating and long walks in the snow; helping on the farms of family and friends, especially at harvest time, and observing pig-killing and bark-harvesting with fascination. These activities were pursued in the company of other boys, while dancing, teas, table games and singing brought together both sexes and all ages. Meanwhile from 1864 to 1868, from the ages of five to nine, he attended Mrs Floyd's first school in Narrow Lane.

The *Reminiscences* contain several references to his Huguenot forebears and, for whatever reason – perhaps merely owing to curiosity about his surname, probably the corrupted version of a French one, descending in the direct male line from the immigrant to the artist – his chronicle reveals a lifelong sense of Huguenot identity.

In 1911, he inquired of the Huguenot Society in London whether any more was known about the surname in London records, as a Huguenot family in Oxfordshire would almost certainly have originally settled in the capital city. He was told that although the name might have 'transmogrified', it seemed almost certainly of French origin. The Shuffreys like other Huguenot refugees used to supplying the more luxurious European textile trade, were skilled craftsmen as well as competent business people, and they integrated with ease in Oxfordshire – at the height of Shuffrey's career the wider family included a well-known Oxford architect Leonard Shuffrey, and Henry Shuffrey, principal cataloguer at the Bodleian Library for sixty-eight years from 1863.

Predisposed to handiwork involving colour and detail, Shuffrey had the good fortune to be sent to a secondary school in Witney (from the ages of nine to fourteen, between 1868 and 1873) *(Plate 5)* offering a weekly class in art provided by a Miss Cropper from Oxford, who trained him in 'sepia', perspective and watercolour. He was later to describe his knowledge of watercolour at the time of his leaving as 'considerable', and as he was not inclined to overstatement, this attests the thoroughness of his instruction. He was also an academically gifted pupil and was prepared for the new Cambridge Local Examinations which he passed in six subjects in 1872 – in fact he was ready to sit the examinations in 1871, a year before he was old enough to do so.

From the age of fourteen he was entirely self-taught, and the *Reminiscences* provide a few inklings of how this was achieved. The value of copying old masters and outstanding works of art is reiterated. Years later, Shuffrey, as painting master in his turn at Summerfields preparatory school in Oxford, instilled this habit in his pupils. One of them, the artist Victor Pasmore, wrote that 'as an art teacher I owe him a great debt because he set a very high standard by encouraging me to copy reproductions of watercolours by great English artists'. This was probably Miss Cropper's approach, and Shuffrey almost certainly continued to follow it after leaving school.

Several of the paintings from the early years of his Oxford career are versions of Oxford views by earlier watercolour artists, especially Peter de Wint, JMW Turner and William Turner of Oxford. A partial record by Shuffrey himself of paintings copied has survived in the form of a handlist of over 500 of his pictures and their measurements, including five entries described as 'after' CJ Adams, Francia, De Wint (*Harvesting* and *Iffley*) and Turner of Oxford (*Oxford from Headington Hill*). The undated picture by Shuffrey, *The River Thames at Iffley* after de Wint (*Plate 7*) is clearly based upon de Wint's watercolour painting entitled *The Village of Iffley near Oxford*, painted before 1834, in the collection of the Ashmolean Museum (*Plate 8*), and probably the one referred to in the handlist. In de Wint's picture the tower of Iffley Church is placed centrally in the composition, with the figures of barge-men and tow-horse, and the barge, balanced to right and left in the middle ground. In the foreground are interesting details of a lock mechanism alongside the curving tow-path which leads the viewer obliquely into the composition. The palette is primarily composed of deep blue- to silver-greens contrasted with secondary reddish tones of the roofs and the deep mahoghany of the horse's coat. A striking feature is the heavy use of scratching out to show the effects of the wind – ripples in the water, and the backs of leaves and grasses whipping over.

Shuffrey's copy could never be mistaken for the original. The impressionistic or even expressionistic human figures obeying no canon of proportions, but suggestive instead of natural shapes in the landscape, and the gentle palette of warm autumnal tones with impressionistic but accurately observed foliage, are entirely characteristic of the later artist. But the adoption of de Wint's viewpoint subtly highlighting the most ancient building in the landscape, of interesting circumstantial details noted in the foreground, and especially of the path curving into the picture, is striking as these are all features frequently seen in Shuffrey's compositions from his Oxford period.

Leaving school at the age of fourteen in 1873, Shuffrey had no easier a transition to his future working life than many a modern school-leaver. His mother had perceived his academic and artistic ability but training through an apprenticeship was beyond the family's means. After the death of his mother in 1875, the sixteen-year-old Shuffrey seemed destined for farming, the occupation which he had been pursuing since leaving school, and this continued until the unanticipated offer of a banking position in 1877 at the age of eighteen. Thus for four formative years Shuffrey was almost exclusively engaged in farming and growing vegetables. True to character, he developed a skill and enthusiasm for these tasks which he retained throughout life, helping to run the Petersfield Horticultural Show from 1887 to 1893 and the Bampton Horticultural Show for three years between 1898 and 1902, and engaging in it again with relish at times of necessity, at Bampton after his early retirement from the bank, and during the First World War at Oxford. His love of gardening and plants generally is apparent in many of the Oxford and Oxfordshire watercolours, for example those of *Ham Court, Bampton (Plate 27)* and *St John's College (Plate 39)*.

The Banking Years

Shuffrey's twenty-year career as clerk and cashier with the London and County Bank was the outcome of a chance meeting, resulting in a rather pompously

Plate 7. The River Thames at Iffley, after de Wint. Watercolour by J.A. Shuffrey. 506 x 330mm. Private collection.

Width is given first, height second, in this and following captions, and all the watercolours that follow are by J.A. Shuffrey.

Plate 8. The Village of Iffley near Oxford. Watercolour by Peter de Wint. Ashmolean Museum WA 1850.89.

conducted interview in which his academic suitability and good deportment ensured success. This career was neither sought by him nor probably much enjoyed (he states in the *Reminiscences* that he has no intention of discussing it), but nevertheless it provided a series of bases in old towns accessible to attractive countryside – first Abingdon from 1877 to 1882, then Arundel from 1882 to 1884, finally Petersfield from 1884 to 1896 – a secure income, and a routine with long summer evenings free to explore picturesque landscapes. All of these gave his artistic talent scope to develop.

Joining the Abingdon branch of the London and County Bank at eighteen, Shuffrey mentions that summer (of 1877) as the time when he began walking to local villages to sketch, so there is certainty that from this time at least he was tackling his own landscape compositions. A remarkable survival, a sketch book now in the manuscript collections of the Bodleian Library, is entitled *Churches of Abingdon & neighbourhood sketched by J Allen Shuffrey in the years 1877-8*. This contains thirty pencil sketches of churches by the late teenager, in which his skills in observation, composition and technique may be seen rapidly developing. One of the earliest pictures, of *Culham Church* dated 1877 in pencil on sketching paper washed over in a pale gold, shows the church from the south-southwest, with a luxuriant creeper scrambling up the tower and the churchyard overgrown *(Plate 12)*. Although technically sound the field is filled with detail and the effect is busy. A pencil sketch of *Cumnor Church* done the following year, 1878, from the south west with the tower in the foreground, shows much more restraint in the use of detail. There is a pleasing balance between architectural and landscape elements (tall trees framing the composition on each side, the broken ground of the churchyard and creepers reclaiming the south side of the church) *(Plate 13)*. The sketches

are all small. Some have been cropped to reach the desired field, but others show increasing control in initial composition, with the church set in a framework composed sometimes of trees (like the sketch dated 1878 of *Sunningwell Church: Plate 14*), sometimes of tombstones, sometimes simply by the artful connection of tussocks and shadows in the churchyard. Experiments in viewpoint include drawing the subject from above (with little success) or, more successfully, from below. For example, *Long Wittenham Church* is shown slightly from below, with the tower in the foreground, off centre and at an angle, while the other elements of the building follow downward to the right like the body of a gigantic animal *(Plate 15)*. The same sketch is one of a number illustrating that the atmospheric effects later to be praised in his watercolours were already apparent in the youthful pencil sketches, where the skilful use of shadow playing over isolated buildings vividly reflects the passing of the late summer afternoon (in fact nearly all the sketches of this period would have been made at the end of a day's work and after an interval of a journey of several miles). The use of trees and shrubs is already confident in these early pictures, and in one, the sketch of *Wootton Church* dated 1878, where a hedge bounding the church curls right across the foreground of the picture from side to side, quite original.

Despite the early facility with a pencil, confidence with watercolours took considerably more working at, as is apparent from a second album in the Bodleian Library. Entitled simply *J Allen Shuffrey*, this contains fifty-seven small-sized watercolour pictures (and an undated landscape sketch, and two photographs, undated, of a calf and some cows!). Many are dated 1879, 1880 and 1881, including eighteen Oxfordshire scenes, of which several are closely similar in composition to the pencil sketches. In one of the best of this group, *The Fish House, Cokethrope, 1879,*

S. HELEN'S, ABINGDON.

Reproduced from a drawing by J. ALLEN SHUFFREY.

Plate 9. St Helen's Church, Abingdon. East St Helen's Street, probably the most interesting in Abingdon, was one of the first medieval streets to be laid out, linking church and marketplace. It preserves a number of fine medieval and later buildings. Drawing, from a postcard 130 x 170mm.

Plate 10. Shuffrey as a young man in the 1870s. Studio photograph by Smith and Hall, Oxford.

Plate 11. The Abingdon branch of the London and County Bank in 1877. The Marketplace frontage of the large late medieval double-gabled townhouse was updated in the later 19th century.

13

areas of fairly basic greens, blues and limestone tones are soft and pale and blend to a degree across the composition. Most of the remainder of the 1879-81 pictures offer an immature palette of blues, greens and red-browns in isolated patches ineptly juxtaposed. However in a picture painted seven years later, a harvest scene dated 1886, huge strides have been made in the use of colour, suggesting that the development of the artist's palette and colour wash technique took place during the years at Arundel. Another striking watercolour from this album, of Stanford-in-the-Vale, is unfortunately undated although likely to belong to the early 1880s.

After five years in Abingdon he was delighted to be moved to the Arundel branch of the bank in 1882. He said it seemed 'selected as the most desirable branch for my art work' - the downland landscape in the vicinity of Arundel must have had an even greater appeal for him than the low-lying agricultural landscape surrounding Abingdon. Several full-sized landscape pictures survive from this period; two are illustrated. One, *Arundel Park* dated 1882 *(Plate 16)*, a pure landscape, is one of a relatively small number of such compositions by the artist. He was making great strides at this time, by his own account in the *Reminiscences*, deriving practical assistance and inspiration from Francis Nicholson's *The Practice of Drawing and Painting Landscape from Nature in Water Colours*, which had been published in 1820 (2nd edition 1823).

Nicholson had introduced his essay as aimed at the 'many persons, of whose education drawing has formed a part, (who) are yet unable to do more than copy the works of others'. The book's sensitive and engaging approach to both subject matter and reader are still charming, and the step-by-step advice still masterly nearly two centuries after publication. To the Oxfordshire country boy turned bank-clerk in rural Sussex, the discovery of this volume must have

been an inestimable boon. Time and time again the gracefully expressed and sensibly structured advice calls to mind particular Shuffrey compositions. Concerning the selection of a subject, 'those are to be preferred that are composed of few parts, and of large forms. The point of view should be where the objects appear to combine together'. Concerning the station or viewpoint, 'it is to be preferred rather low than otherwise'. Regarding how much to sketch, 'particular notice should be taken of the objects terminating the view at each end'. Regarding the depiction of foliage, where the young Shuffrey struggled according to his own account, 'the character and lightness of foliage depending very much upon the touch and execution, more particularly at the extremities, it is very necessary for the learner to acquire a good touch of the pencil, which should be done in some measure previously to the study of nature'. Shuffrey singled out one area of instruction for particular acknowledgement, the 'processes in colouring . . . the easiest . . . consist(ing) in making out with greys the effect of light and shadow, and in adding the colours upon it'. The use to which he put it may be observed in a number of his unfinished pictures.

The second picture from the Arundel period illustrated here, *Bignor near Arundel* dated 1885 *(Plate 17)*, is of interest as an early example of a subject to which the artist returned throughout his career – the ancient timber-framed dwelling. Before the gentrification of the countryside, antique buildings had not yet become desirable residences, and were often in a state of gentle and gradual deterioration of great appeal to the landscape artist. Shuffrey clearly regarded old timber-framed buildings as organic elements in the landscape, often as here placing them off-centre or at an angle rather than letting them dominate the field. The depiction of the Wealden-style house at Bignor is still hesitant.

But his picture, also dated 1885, of the 17th century manor house at Denchworth near Witney *(Plate 20)*, the home of his bride Esther Walker, fully captures Shuffrey's fascination with the ancient timber-framing beneath uneven roofs, the medley of building materials, and windows and door all of different dates and at different alignments. This sympathy for timber-framed structures was eventually to express itself as one of the most striking characteristics of the long series of Oxford townscapes, and the artist returned to the same theme in his final years when sketching in the Oxfordshire countryside.

From 1884 to 1896 Shuffrey was based at the Bank's Petersfield branch. Despite his lack of enthusiasm for banking work, he appears to have handled it in exemplary fashion, and was promoted on at least one occasion. His competence as an organiser is witnessed by the number of local groups in his towns of residence who sought him out as committee member or even as secretary. In Petersfield, for example, he became Honorary Secretary of both the Church of England Temperance Society and the Petersfield Horticultural Show. Long after the end of his banking career, his clerical skills were in evidence in the book-keeping relating to his painting, and in the financial acumen, it could be argued, shown by his handling of his painting career generally.

The immediate background to his retirement from the bank in 1897 was a long absence brought on by chill and fever. But he was also becoming increasingly concerned about the deterioration of his eyesight. This was compounded by a move to the Romford branch in 1896, where his position as Cashier 'made a very long day at the counter'. Anxiety that his ability to continue painting could suffer permanently may well have led to the headaches and illnesses he experienced in his last years with the bank.

Bampton

Obliged to rebuild his career after early retirement from the bank owing to illness, Shuffrey and his wife and young family returned in the 1890s to the Witney area, settling at Bampton in 1898.

The family network was invaluable in helping him to make this difficult transition. His brother Leonard offered the family temporary tenancy of the Old Farmhouse in Woodgreen, which had a large garden where Shuffrey grew vegetables and kept fowls. The two children attended schools in Witney, where Shuffrey rediscovered childhood connections who helped him to obtain the position of drawing master to five young ladies being schooled at the Vicarage in Bampton. It was about this time that he adopted a tricycle as the principal mode of transport for his work.

Bampton in 1898 was an attractive country town, in former times an important commercial centre but now in the course of eclipse by Witney and Oxford. Shuffrey had noticed the low price of houses there. When Leonard required the return of the Old Farmhouse in 1898 pending his son's marriage, Shuffrey bought The Laurels just north of Bampton and the family lived there for four years between 1898 and 1902.

Shuffrey continued to garden and was soon 'persuaded' to become Secretary to the Bampton Horticultural Show. He also quickly began to take artistic advantage of the attractions of the local landscape; the picture of *St Mary's Bampton (Plate 26)* appears to have been painted shortly after the family's removal in 1898. He mentions doing 'a good many water colours of beauty spots near', and sending them to two successive Oxford Art Society exhibitions in 1898 and 1900 where the majority were almost certainly sold. (This auspicious beginning was to be followed by a long series of exhibitions in

Plate 12. Culham, 1877, from *Churches of Abingdon & neighbourhood sketched by J Allen Shuffrey in the years 1877-8.* Bodleian Library.

The pages of this early sketchbook were colour-washed in various pale colours by the young artist.

Plate 13. Cumnor, 1878, from *Churches of Abingdon & neighbourhood sketched by J Allen Shuffrey in the years 1877-8.* Bodleian Library.

Plate 14. Sunningwell, 1878, from *Churches of Abingdon & neighbourhood sketched by J Allen Shuffrey in the years 1877-8.* Bodleian Library.

Plate 15. Long Wittenham, from *Churches of Abingdon & neighbourhood sketched by J Allen Shuffrey in the years 1877-8.* Bodleian Library.

Plate 16. Arundel Park, 1882.
Watercolour 355 x 240mm.
Private collection.

Plate 17. Bignor near Arundel, 1885. Watercolour 456 x 292mm. Private collection.

Oxford as well as in London, the artist diligently saving both sales catalogues and reviews.)

Fortunately several pictures from these years survive in private collections. Four illustrated here show Shuffrey tackling village landscapes in Bampton and the surrounding area *(Plates 24-27)*. Village churches are added to the repertoire, typically focussing on the medieval stone spire accompanied by the fine old trees to be found at the centre of the village, which are often allowed to obscure the church building itself. The artist had become interested in the medieval origins of villages and was developing an eye for peculiarities like the long green stretching north from St Mary's in Witney *(Plate 25)*, the remains of the Anglo-Saxon minster enclosure surrounding St Mary's, Bampton *(Plate 26)*, and the fragment of 14th century castle gateway and battlements at the core of Ham Court, Bampton *(Plate 27)*. All these developing interests would be explored further in Oxford.

Oxford

In the autumn of 1902 Shuffrey and his family moved to Oxford, his base and principal artistic theme for the remainder of his life and career. The account given in the *Reminiscences* of the move and its background is somewhat disjointed. The final summer in Bampton had been a difficult one for the family, which now included a two-year-old daughter Dora, born in 1900. Smallpox broke out in the town and there were fatalities. Social and commercial life appears to have broken down completely for several months, and even church services ceased. The family, fortunately located north of central Bampton, kept going by drinking the milk of their goats but they had to travel north and east to Brize Norton and Witney for bread and meat.

Up to this time, Shuffrey and his wife had always lived in relatively small country towns, and when possible, in countryside locations on their edges. But the situation in the final year at Bampton may have predisposed Shuffrey to consider positively a radically different alternative which now presented itself as a direct result of the two exhibitions in Oxford and his election to membership of the Oxford Art Society.

His work had clearly been appreciated, both artistically and in terms of sales, at these Oxford exhibitions. The blend of buildings and landscape in which he specialised had long been popular among topographical artists and connoisseurs in Oxford. His name was becoming known by word of mouth, and he was recommended by the Secretary of the Oxford Art Society to Canon Kennard of Christ Church for a private commission with which the Canon was extremely pleased. Supporters in Bampton and Oxford now urged him to move to the city and paint the colleges, work for which there was a growing market.

Consequently in the autumn of 1902 the family left West Oxfordshire for a townhouse in Thorncliffe Road just south of Summertown, and two miles north of central Oxford. The house was spacious but the small town garden would not permit gardening on a scale sufficient to supplement their diet or income, marking a turning-point in his career after which the family would be more dependent upon his making a financial success of his art. A final exhibition in Bampton of his recent pictures provided a favourable omen. Attendance was good despite an entry charge ('to be given to the Vicar for the School fund') and sales of pictures earned the artist more than £20, a substantial sum when it is recalled that the house at Bampton had only cost ten times that much four years previously.

The move was thus a professional one and involved embracing the requirements of the burgeoning Oxford art market. Among these were picture postcards, especially ones with a topographical theme. In 1904 Shuffrey was commissioned by the Oxford firm of Robert Peel to produce a series of six pictures of stained glass windows in the Cathedral which were also published as postcards and also in a book of Oxford views. There followed further postcard commissions from Alden & Co, Oxford and from Faulkner & Co, London. These last were widely distributed, so that Shuffrey himself was soon in a position to publish his own series, using Mowbray & Co. The four postcards illustrated *(Plates 42-45)*, all dated 1904, include both images based on his large-scale work (he mentions using 'six printed from my best large pictures' for the Mowbray series) like the postcard of *All Souls College (Plate 42)*; the more miniaturist style used for the original Peel commission, exemplified by the postcard of the 17th century *Jonah Window, Christ Church Cathedral (Plate 45)*, and two views in a very abbreviated style with sharp light contrast which must have been designed solely for the postcard market, the postcard of *Corpus Christi College (Plate 43)* and the postcard of *Magdalen Bridge and Magdalen College (Plate 44)*. As a result of the commercial success and wide distribution of these printed images, Shuffrey was known primarily as a postcard artist for many years after his death.

Another immediate outcome of the move to Oxford which had long-term consequences was the extension of his work as an art teacher. His initial drawing class may have met at his house, but as 'lessons continued' he took a room at 6 High Street. Soon he was teaching the young ladies of families resident both at Christ Church and Stanton Harcourt Manor. In 1912 he was asked to give twice-weekly drawing and sepia lessons to pupils at Summerfields preparatory school in Summertown. He continued to do so until 1930, and he speaks with pride in the *Reminiscences* of boys he had taught who then went on to distinguish themselves.

Plate 18. The Laurels, Bampton *c* 1898, with James, Esther, Reginald and Babs.

Plate 19. Esther at Denchworth Manor with Reginald, c 1888.

Plate 20. Denchworth Manor, 1885. The four-bay house is of the 17th century, with an 18th century shell-canopy over the doorway and reset 15th century moulding in the ground floor window. Childhood home of Shuffrey's wife Esther. Watercolour 360 x 255mm. Private collection.

Plate 21. Shuffrey and Esther as newlyweds in the 1880s.

Plate 22. Dora Shuffrey, born 1900, aged about six. This photograph was probably taken by Shuffrey's friend Jones, on a Lumiere Autochrome plate. These plates used one of the earliest colour processes with dyed starch grains.

Plate 23. Barbara Shuffrey, born 1892, aged about eight.

Shuffrey and Oxford Topographical Art

An evaluation of Shuffrey's 'Oxford' art would be impossible without reference to the series of Oxford artists from Malchair to Buckler, and including especially Rooker, JMW Turner and William Turner of Oxford, whose works would have been accessible to him to a greater or lesser degree in the collections of the Ashmolean Museum and Bodleian Library, and particularly in the engravings published annually in the Oxford University Almanack.

A recent review of Oxford topographical art before Malchair has shown how early modern city mapping, Oxford printing and the University's fame, architectural significance and increasing generation of tourism, was the background to Malchair's establishment in the second half of the 18th century as unofficial University drawing master and recorder of ancient Oxford buildings scheduled for demolition (Julian Munby, 'Malchair and the Oxford Topographical Tradition', in Colin Harrison, *John Malchair of Oxford*, Oxford 1998). The new landscape art of this period reflects both the awareness of decay and loss of structures from former periods amounting almost to a cult of ruins, and the new aesthetic ideal of the Picturesque, a deliberate move away from the previously popular Allegorical landscape to one in which the elements are made to seem the happy result of accidental juxtaposition (Patrick Connor, *Michael Angelo Rooker 1746-1801*, London 1984, 63).

Arriving in England from Germany about 1754 and settling in Oxford in 1759, Malchair was largely self-taught, and developed a soft, suggestive style of painting based upon pencil sketching combined with grey and later watercolour washes, which he combined with eccentric viewpoints in an unconventional style. During the 1770s and 1780s he was active in Oxford recording ancient and picturesque views soon to be swept away as a consequence of the Mileways Acts. His artistic influence survived into the 19th century in the work of successive Oxford drawing masters and in the important Wellesley collection, parts of which were sold to Corpus Christi College about 1850 and to the Ashmolean Museum in 1928 (Harrison, *Malchair*, 16-28).

A comparison of Shuffrey's Oxford views with those of Malchair suggests some similarities which seem more than accidental, both generally, in the soft style combining pencil and watercolour washes and the personal and unusual choice of viewpoints down alley-ways and into back courts, and specifically, in the case of several paintings. Shuffrey's *Stable Yard, North Side of Holywell Street, 1907 (Plate 49)*, like Malchair's *The Stable Yard at Merton College* (1775) (Harrison, *Malchair*, 77-8, Cat. 20), shows an empty sunlit yard, with minimal details (in Malchair's case, a drain and a sheaf, in Shuffrey's, some cobbles and a ladder and bucket), absolutely quiet, without figures or action, yet soaked in the atmosphere of everyday life. There is a high but hazy contrast of light and shade; in Malchair's picture one looks across the yard toward a shadowed coach gate, while in Shuffrey's, one looks into the yard through a comparable gate. Shuffrey's two pictures of 1908 and 1912 of *The Turf Inn* and *New College Bell Tower (Plates 50, 52)*, like Malchair's *Merton Tower from Magpie Lane* (1776) (Harrison, *Malchair*, 81 Cat. 25), show a college tower centrally overlooking a sharply narrowing alley-way, on the left ancient cottages with windows thrown open, on the right a blank wall overhung by trees. The scene is empty and quiet, with just the suggestion of daily life in the form of a woman's bonneted profile in an upper window (Malchair) and wash hanging out to dry (Shuffrey).

Malchair's moment of public fame came briefly when his pictures were selected as the basis for engravings for the *Oxford Almanack* in 1768/69. Thereafter for twenty years the Almanack used the views of London artist, engraver and scene-painter Michael Angelo Rooker. Rooker, a distinguished architectural draughtsman and leader in the development of the new art of watercolour, quickly established a new canon for *Oxford Almanack* illustrations of the city which was followed until the 20th century. The principal features of his pattern are a University building, often new but if not, drawn as if new, shown at an oblique angle, with great attention to architectural detail, conspicious gardens and foliage, a large and lively staffage reminiscent of Dutch 17th century painting, and marginal glimpses of other Oxford landmarks to set the subject into context (Connor, *Michael Angelo Rooker*, 106-110). Although the twenty *Almanack* engravings would have been readily accessible to Shuffrey, only one, *Magdalen College with the Old Bridge*, designed for the *Almanack* of 1771 (Connor, Rooker, 112 fig. 62), appears to have inspired the later artist. The comparison with Shuffrey's *Horse-drawn Carriages on Magdalen Bridge* of the early 1900s *(Plate 35)* serves to highlight the differences, as well as the similarities, in approach. Rooker uses a horizontal format, Shuffrey an upright. In both the Tower is placed centrally in the middle ground, viewed from the east by Rooker, from the west by Shuffrey. Rooker's emphasis is on architectural detail, the buildings are depicted as if new and in perfect condition, and the Picturesque element is supplied by lively foreground staffage, including a coach. Shuffrey's treatment is soft, with gentle colours and alternation of light and shade; the few figures included are subordinated to the prolific early autumn foliage, but the timely inclusion of a tramcar suggests a reference to the *Almanack* picture.

Even as Rooker was working on the last of his views for the *Oxford Almanack*, JMW Turner, the child prodigy destined to become England's greatest painter, was studying Rooker's Oxford work closely, as illustrated by his competent copy of Rooker's *Friar Bacon's Study* painted in watercolours at the age of twelve (Colin Harrison, *Turner's Oxford*, Ashmolean Museum, 2000, 38). Although Turner never lived in Oxford he had a number of useful local connections and made numerous pictures of the city between the 1780s and 1830s, supplying ten images to the *Oxford Almanack* between 1799 and 1811 (Harrison, *Turner's Oxford*, 61-75).

Turner was a restlessly experimental technician, adding pen and ink outlines and white bodycolour to the by now standard watercolour technique of pencil and wash, and pushing to their limits liberties taken with viewpoint and proportion to create dramatic images, large in scope, of famous University buildings. Seen as 'modern' architecture, these are often still in the throes of creation - a deliberately startling and arresting vision of traditional Oxford, the Picturesque tourist destination.

All Turner's *Almanack* illustrations would have been readily available to Shuffrey, and the original paintings of a number of them had been in the collections of the Ashmolean Museum since 1850. Shuffrey copied one of these, *A View of the Inside of Brazen Nose College Quadrangle*, engraved for the *Almanack* in 1805 (Harrison, *Turner's Oxford*, 24, Pl. 16, Cat. 44) for his 1904 postcard *Brasenose College (Plate 113)*. The arresting viewpoint, the relationships of the college and University buildings, with the dome of the Radcliffe Camera and the spire of St Mary-the-Virgin Church looming, like tall ships riding in harbour, against a dramatic sky are Turner's. So is the use of sunlight and shade to punctuate the march of the mullions of the Quad's unusual dormer windows

Plate 24. Yelford Manor, near Witney. The view of this fine late medieval timber-framed house on a moated site accentuates the low-lying character of the landscape. Probably painted in the 1890s. Watercolour 375 x 221mm. Private collection.

Plate 25. St Mary's Witney, 1896. The town church and churchyard, viewed from the Green at a carefully selected angle, have a village aspect. Watercolour 456 x 305mm. Private collection.

Plate 26. St Mary's, Bampton, 1898. One of the oldest and most interesting churches in Oxfordshire, built on the site of an Anglo-Saxon minster, the line of whose banked enclosure, partly preserved as the churchyard, forms the centre of the composition. Watercolour 456 x 355mm. Private collection.

Plate 27. Ham Court, Bampton. In the centre are the medieval gatehouse and the last standing fragment of the parapet wall of the massive 14th century Bampton Castle. Probably painted in the 1890s. Watercolour 368 x 260mm. Private collection.

Plate 28. Wadham College, Parks Road, 1902. One of Oxford's first motorcars is gently introduced into an otherwise timeless presentation. Watercolour used as a postcard in 1904, 366 x 268mm. OXCMS:2002.74.3.

Plate 29. Tom Tower, Oxford. Christ Church's outstanding landmark was designed by Christopher Wren for Dean Fell in 1681. The view selected from the quiet collegiate street opposite detaches the building from its location on the downward slope of bustling St Aldate's. Pencil drawing. Private collection.

Plate 30. Shuffrey painting in the gardens of St John's College *c* 1903. He is sitting in the garden northeast of Canterbury Quad and is using what appears to be a collapsible easel and chair combination.

horizontally across the mid-line of the composition. However inspection of the site itself reveals exaggeration and distortion by the earlier artist in the interests of creating a dramatic image, with the north and south ranges of the quadrangle spread beyond their limits, so that the foreground has lost all reality. Shuffrey's copy clearly involved a visit to the site to correct the proportions of the tiny quadrangle and garden, incidentally establishing a more genuine as well as a more subtle distinction between the small scale of college life in the cosy quadrangle and the larger, grander University buildings outside its confines. If Turner's original has the appearance of a brilliantly lit stage set, Shuffrey's picture is most definitely a landscape. To quote a review of 1906, 'the manner in which (Shuffrey) gets his atmospheric effects is particularly fine, and this is seen not only in the landscapes, but also in a picture such as that of Brasenose' (*Fine Art Trade Journal*, October 1906).

A second Almanack view by Turner which may have influenced Shuffrey is that for 1806, *View of Exeter College, All Saints Church &c from the Turl* (Harrison, *Turner's Oxford,* 25, Pl. 17, Cat. 45). Here an exaggerated perspective has made a small road immensely wide and long and the church spire both lofty and distant; building works dominate the foreground. Shuffrey's vision of the same street, *The Turl, Oxford,* selects a vantage point halfway down the street which is cloaked in a warm, sleepy autumnal atmosphere, and puts the old houses, college buildings and church in their correct proportions and relationships – a return to the Picturesque.

Just a year before the appearance of Turner's final *Almanack* contribution in 1811, another talented young watercolour artist finished his apprenticeship in London. This was William Turner of Oxford, who although hailed as a prodigy in his teenage years, turned his back on the London art scene at the age of twenty and returned to Oxford to paint his native county with little recognition in his lifetime (Timothy Wilcox, Christopher Titterington, *William Turner of Oxford*, Oxfordshire County Museum Service, 1984). Dedicated to landscape, Turner of Oxford saw nature as a source of moral values, its forces larger than man and his works, and the landscape picture as a means of conveying a message beyond the mere love of ruins and the picturesque. Turner of Oxford was collected enthusiastically by the Morrell family in Oxford, whose St Giles home was the scene in 1925 of a massive sale of his pictures, a collection which may have been known to members of the Oxford Art Society much earlier.

Although his contribution to the depiction of the Oxford urban scene was relatively negligible, Turner of Oxford's wonderful, rather disturbing views of neighbouring places such as Stanton Harcourt, Combe, Wychwood, Shotover and Hinksey may have influenced Shuffrey in his own portrayal of the city's suburbs. *A Quarry near Shotover*, painted around 1818 (Wilcox, Titterington, *William Turner of Oxford*, 46 Cat. 35) dramatises the intrusion of the industrial landscape as a 'pale rent . . . in the dark hillside'. Shuffrey depicts a clay quarry not dissimilarly in Summertown Brickworks, where the dark hole of the quarry and tall stack contrast with an otherwise mellow agricultural landscape, and the sultry pinks of the sunset over Wytham suggest the heat of the kilns. Shuffrey's *Oxford from North Hinksey*, a theme treated by nearly all the Oxford artists under discussion here, is closest in viewpoint and composition to Turner of Oxford's *Oxford from Hinksey Hill* (Wilcox, Titterington, *William Turner of Oxford*, 35 Cat. 16) in its vision of the town strung along the horizon to the right, with foreground trees to the left and the sinuous curve of the road down into the floodplain.

A close contemporary of Turner of Oxford was John Chessell Buckler, an architectural draughtsman and architect who succeeded to his father's practice, having also received lessons in watercolour from Francis Nicholson (JC Buckler, *Drawings of Oxford, 1811-1827*, Bodleian Library, 1951, Introduction). These sepia drawings of Oxford buildings presented to the Bodleian in 1929 include a number of views also used by Shuffrey, for example, Littlemore Hall, St Aldate's, 1811, All Saints Church from Turl Street, 1824, and Oriel College, from Kybald Street, 1822 (Buckler, *Drawings of Oxford*, 2, 10, 12). With his penchant for picturesque compositions and his interest in courts and side streets, Buckler's work could have served as a general starting-point for the later artist if accessible before 1929. In this context it is perhaps significant that a relative of the artist, Henry Joseph Shuffrey, had worked at the Bodleian Library since 1863. A library publication of 1907 describes him as a Senior Assistant with responsibility for the upkeep and updating of the library's pre-1920 catalogue (*Supplement to the Staff Calendar, Bodleian Library, 1907*, p. 31). Having almost certainly joined the library direct from school (he worked there altogether for 58 years), he reached the highest position possible for a staff member not entering as an academic curator (information kindly provided by Mr Steven Tomlinson, Post medieval Manuscripts, Bodleian Library), and would have been an extremely useful contact for the artist.

Shuffrey never mentions studying published sources or museum or private collections as inspiration for his Oxford views, but his surviving pictures make it clear that considerable research was carried out once he had arrived in Oxford. It has been demonstrated that he made a study of the *Almanack* views, and studied the colour original in the Ashmolean Museum when he decided to make a direct copy. But he was little influenced by the *Almanack* as a whole, and not in sympathy with the Rooker 'canon' – highly detailed studies of new buildings combined with formal, detailed studies of trees and gardens – which dominated the *Almanack* into the 20th century.

As a watercolour painter he was personally attracted rather to the earlier, classic period of watercolour painting of the late 18th and early 19th centuries, represented technically by Francis Nicholson and his publication of 1823. This embodied the Picturesque ideal of the later 18th century: a consciousness of decay and romanticisation of ruins, an accidental-seeming juxtaposition of elements, and especially a strong landscape context for buildings and structures which are seen as integral landscape elements. He also adhered closely to the classic technique of pencil sketching and watercolour wash, without use of bodycolour or brush drawing.

The Picturesque idea of populating the foreground of a topographical landscape with human figures ('staffage') engaged in lively, everyday pursuits was a development of late 17th century and later Dutch painting which depicts townscapes filled with the activities of the middle and lower classes. Oxford topographical art continued the tradition, but individual artists made use of staffage very variously. Rooker's staffage remains truest to type, JMW Turner's most eccentric (the figures seen in earlier pictures, often engaged in monumental building works, disappear altogether later), Buckler's is minimal and rather uninteresting, while Turner of Oxford uses occasional figures symbolically. Shuffrey's use of staffage is closest to Malchair's in being minimal, understated and apparently classless – it doesn't seem important whether the men and women by the colleges or in the street are college servants, dons and their wives, or even tourists.

Related to staffage in the Picturesque ideal are props, redolent of recent activitiy which has only just ceased.

Just as JMW Turner selected equipment bearing on his own particular interest, the idea of Oxford in the process of being built in stone, Shuffrey highlights things to do with his own particular interest, gardening, showing every college building balanced by lush foliage, and pots of flowers and tiny borders in the meanest court, and well tended vegetables in the cottage gardens.

Shuffrey was apparently little influenced by contemporary Oxford topographical art of the early years of the 20th century. Two pictures of 1902 by the most comparable contemporary artist EA Phipson, *Littlemore Court* and *George Street* (Malcolm Graham *Images of Victorian Oxford*, Sutton 1992, passim) depict similar subject matter to *Plates 55 and 59* but with a remarkably distinct approach.

On the other hand, Shuffrey, himself a keen amateur photographer, must have been familiar with the work of Oxford photographer Henry Taunt. Despite the difference in medium, Taunt's views of Oxford, for example that of shops in Broad Street dated 1875, of Magdalen College Tower dated 1907, of High Street dated 1887 and especially of Upper Fisher Row of about 1875 (Malcolm Graham *Henry Taunt of Oxford. A Victorian Photographer,* The Oxford Illustrated Press, 1973, 4, and passim) with their eccentric viewpoints, interest in light and shade, lush foliage and vehicles, and tendency to view streets and buildings obliquely, may well have influenced Shuffrey's Oxford work in its early stages.

The Oxford Years

The principal reason for moving to Oxford had been to 'paint the Colleges'. He lost no time in settling down to this task, and in bringing to bear on it the blend of landscape and topographical elements so much a part of the Oxford topographical tradition. *Wadham College, Parks Road*, dated 1902 *(Plate 28)* captures the leisurely grace of the southern end of this road. The viewpoint is chosen to include a distant glimpse of the skyline of All Souls, centrally juxtaposing a raking view of the college's main entrance with an early motorcar parked outside it (the viewer wonders – whose?). *St Johns College Garden (Plate 39)*, undated but presumably the result of the painting session recorded in the photograph of about 1903 *(Plate 30)*, captures the impression of an English country house obtained from the college's extensive garden. Two views of the Magdalen College bell tower probably also date from his early years in Oxford - one includes an Oxford tramcar *(Plate 35)*, the other shows the tower rising spectrally beyond the principal gateway of the Botanical Gardens *(Plate 119)*.

The progress of Shuffrey's career in Oxford soon fulfilled the hopes and expectations of 1902. Renting a studio in central Oxford from 1906, he notes that 'at times we had quite a number of visitors – a great many Americans and foreigners', and production of desirable Oxford views had to keep pace accordingly. Fortunately he seems never to have created a picture without imbuing it with a charm and interest of his own making, during the Oxford years adding to his previous themes a curiosity about the contemporary uses of buildings of former grandeur, and a determination to record ancient structures scheduled for demolition, both very much in the Malchair tradition.

Examples of what reviewers dubbed his 'disappearing Oxford' pictures include *Two Views of Octagon House, Catte Street (Plates 56, 57), Broad Street, Bliss Court (Plate 54), Botley Mill dated 1907 (Plate 69), Two Views of Iffley Mill (Plates 70, 71), Summertown Brickworks (Plate 73), Three Views of Fisher Row (Plates*

Plates 31, 32 and 33. Shuffrey became a keen amateur photographer. These three photographs, made into lantern slides, of seasonal farming occupations – sowing, threshing, and making hayricks (with daughter Dora on left) – were taken by him in 1906 at Cogges near Witney. Farming had barely changed between Shuffrey's childhood and the First World War.

Plate 34. Witney Feast Fair in the late 19th century.

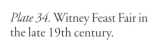

78, 79 80) and *Two Views of Oxford Castle and Mill dated 1912 (Plates 80, 81)*. Although not all these 'last' opportunities were intentional (Iffley Mill was accidentally destroyed by fire shortly after Shuffrey painted it), his eye for what he refers to in the *Reminiscences* as the charming and picturesque repeatedly drew him to paint buildings without a future.

As has been shown, Shuffrey was interested in relatively mean dwellings, and in people's ability to cope, and especially to grow things, in and around them under circumscribed conditions, drawing him to record alleyways and back streets which later were so often prime candidates for demolition, for example the carefully tended little garden in the mean court (*Littlemore Court, St Aldates*, dated 1914, *Plate 55*, the narrow court with flowerpots on a windowsill (*Broad Street, Bliss Court, Plate 54*), Fisher Row with lads fishing in the Castle Mill stream (*Oxford Castle and Mill*, 1912, *Plate 82*).

He had a passion for being productive, which may also have drawn him to particular subjects in the series of pictures of Oxford suburbs – watermills in Botley and Iffley (although these abound in Picturesque art), and the old brickworks in Summertown *(Plate 73)*. Like the Dutch genre painters of the 17th century whose pictures he could have studied in the Ashmolean Museum, he also found charm and interest in Oxford's old public houses many decades before they gained the 'heritage' status which they currently enjoy - *The Turf Inn (Plate 51)*, *The Plough Inn (Plate 83)*, *The Lamb and Flag (Plate 84)* illustrated here are just a few of the large group of Oxford public houses whose pictures he painted.

When in 1934 he made a gift of fifty paintings and drawings to the public of Oxford, a unique collection was created, a study of which explains the rapture with which contemporary Oxford critics often received his exhibited work. Two Oxford pictures seem to sum up his contribution.

In *St Mary the Virgin South Porch (Plate 116)*, a striking composition challenges the viewer simultaneously to appreciate an impressionistic treatment of luxuriant foliage in the limpid light of a watery atmosphere, and a bold rendition of Oxford's most famous piece of baroque architecture. With an unusual perspective diminishing to the right, three successive building periods at St Mary's are treated partly like successive grounds in a landscape, partly like a series of theatrical backdrops.

The foreground subject, the south porch of the medieval church as redesigned by Nicholas Stone in 1637, is the oldest, while in the middle and back grounds are the Victorian parapets and tower redesigned by Scott and punctuated by ghosts of Gothic crockets.

The porch with its twisted columns reminiscent of Bernini's canopy at St Peter's in Rome, and statue of Virgin and Child thrust into a superstructure of wildly competing classical and Renaissance elements, was intensely controversial in its day on the eve of the English Civil War. It epitomises former religious conflicts which the artist now presents as part of the Oxford landscape.

In *Magdalen College: Southwest Corner of the Great Quad (Plate 117)*, the view selected depicts most of the late 15th century structures of the original college, from the left, the Hall, Chapel with bell tower behind and south Cloister range before, and turning the corner, the Antechapel, vestibule and Founder's Tower. But the architectural statement is animated by dramatic suggestion. Blue-green toning of the

Plate 35. Horse-drawn carriages on Magdalen Bridge. The carriages referred to in the title are tramcars of the City of Oxford Tramways Company which opened a tram route from the railway station to the Cowley Road in 1881 (*VCH IV*, 359). By 1910 the majority of trams were double-decker ones as seen here crossing Magdalen Bridge under Magdalen's late medieval Bell Tower. The tram tracks sweep from centre foreground towards the Plain and the Victoria Fountain of 1899 in the distance. Probably painted in the early 1900s. Watercolour. Private collection.

J Allen Shuffrey

Plate 36. The Turl, Oxford. The view south down Turl Street seems to capture the essence of the quiet Collegiate life. Still half in early morning shadow, one side is lined by Lincoln College, the other by University shops accommodated in 17th and 18th century buildings. At the vanishing point is the projecting tower of All Saints church, 'one of the most perfect English churches of its date' – 1706/8 (Pevsner and Sherwood, *Oxfordshire*, 288). Watercolour. Private collection.

Plate 37. Petersfield Jubilee Mug designed by Shuffrey. Petersfield Historical Society.

Plate 38. Whitley near Petersfield. Watercolour 368 x 266mm. Private collection.

Plate 39. Garden, St John's College. The view of the northeast corner of Canterbury Quad with its impressively eclectic three-story collegiate ranges of the 1630s shows the gardens in riotous, undergraduate-free, late summer bloom. Watercolour. Private collection.

foliage and the length and direction of shadow indicate a very early morning in spring, when the opalescent light already bathing the bell tower - the destination of Magdalen choristers on May Day at sunrise - has just lit and seemingly brought to life the figures of actors and musicians surmounting the buttresses. If the picture was meant to depict May morning in Oxford, it is arguably a most subtle and dramatic treatment of the subject, and done without the use of a single living figure.

The Oxfordshire Pictures

For the period after the early years of the 20th century, the time when Shuffrey became a professional painter residing in Oxford, the character of the *Reminiscences* changes. The tragic end of his first marriage, the intervening years and the joyous circumstances of his second marriage having been described in some detail, personal and family life do not feature to the same degree as before. From 1908 the account turns to the annual sketching tours, including the abortive Continental tour in 1914 on the eve of the First World War. Apart from some details of everyday life in Oxford during the 1914-18 war, little more is recounted that does not concern Art Society membership and activities, and exhibitions.

The *Reminiscences* give us few details about the years following the First World War. But a fresh series of paintings and drawings show that throughout his 60s and 70s he was at work in the villages of Oxfordshire, especially those accessible on the routes of the buses of the City of Oxford Motor Services. Shuffrey had made the acquaintance of Arthur Tyler, Director of the company, who asked him to illustrate the publication *Rural Oxford. Sketches of Picturesque and Interesting places on the Motor Bus Routes in the Country Districts around Oxford*, a publication including twenty-eight pencil sketches of Oxfordshire villages which appeared under his name in 1934. According to a review of the same year, 'for many years he has been making a series of sketches of the villages around Oxford (upward of 100) many of which are in the *Bus Guide*.'

Using the skills of an artist to publicise public transport was not a new idea. As early as 1908 when Frank Pick was appointed Assistant Director to the London Underground with responsibility for publicity, artists had been recruited (in that instance, John Hassall, who had already worked in the same capacity for Great Eastern Railways) to stimulate city dwellers to make leisure journeys on public transport. The London Underground initiative resulted in the famous series of 'Metroland' posters (information from Jonathan Riddell, Curator of Ephemera and Posters, London Transport Museum).

The series of watercolour pictures of Oxfordshire villages dating to the 1920s and 1930s *(Plates 92-102, 114)* show that Shuffrey was already engaged upon sketching in Oxfordshire, undoubtedly making use himself of the public bus service - a keen, indeed prodigious cyclist in his youth, he mentions the railways for longer journeys and would naturally have explored the new bus routes as these expanded. Comparison of the sketches published in 1934 with the watercolours show several identical views, that of *Chalgrove (Plate 96)* and the *George Hotel, Dorchester (Plate 99)* and a number of different views of the same villages *(Adderbury, Plate 115* and *Dorchester, Plate 98)*. Where they vary, the 'Bus Guide' views are more obvious ones of High Streets and village landmarks, especially the parish church and tower, while the watercolours continue the exploration of more unusual viewpoints, as in *Old Cottages at Radley (Plate 97)*, *Almshouses at Ewelme (Plate 102)* and *Combe, Woodstock (Plate 114)*.

Plate 40. Arncliffe Vicarage, 1904. Painted on the occasion of the artist's visit in 1904. Watercolour 443 x 266mm. Private collection.

Plate 41. St Oswald's church, Arncliffe, 1904. The stream mentioned in the *Reminiscences* – the River Skirfare - lies just behind the church. Watercolour 443 x 266mm. Private collection.

Plate 42. Postcard of *All Souls College, 1904.* Composition and style are those of the artist's larger compositions, with two of Oxford's famous towers, St Mary the Virgin and the Radcliffe Camera, floating majestically just beyond the confines of the smaller-scale college quadrangle. The wide-angle view chosen, looking west from inside North Quad, focuses the viewer's attention on Hawksmoor's miniature but fantastic design of screen and gatehouse, whose Romantic qualities are emphasised by a lush creeper. From a watercolour. OXCMS:2002.74.93.2.

Plate 43. Postcard of *Corpus Christi College, 1904.* Composition and style have apparently been influenced by the intended publication as a postcard. A narrow vertical slice of the college's 16th century Front Quad confines attention to the gate tower and famous sundial topped by a pelican; shadow and sunlight contrast sharply. From a watercolour. OXCMS:2002.74.94.6.

Plate 44. Postcard of *Magdalen Bridge, Magdalen College, 1904*. An even more obviously simplified composition for the postcard market. Magdalen Bell Tower is just off centre with Magdalen Bridge vanishing towards it in a straight line reflected by the edges of trees opposite; the line of the grassy shore closes the triangle with punters moving straight across in the foreground. Strong contrast is used for stonework, foliage and water. FL Griggs used the same composition but without punts in 'Magdalen Tower', published as a collotype in the *Oxford Almanack* for 1923, based on a pencil drawing dated 1922. From a watercolour. Private collection.

Plate 45. Postcard of the *Jonah Window, Christ Church Cathedral, 1904*. The Jonah window, signed and dated Abraham van Linge 163? (Pevsner and Sherwood, 80), is the west window in the north aisle of the nave, situated between the western, public entrance to the Cathedral and the private entrance from the Deanery garden. Jonah seated beneath the gourd fills the left-hand light and the city of Nineveh mounts up on the right. The intensity of the imaginary Biblical landscape dominates the composition. From a watercolour dated 1903. OXCMS:2002.74.92.5.

Plate 46. Holywell Street, North side, Old houses, 1906. Holywell Street represents one of the most perfect survivals of the 17th century period of expansion in Oxford, with its proliferation of tall, narrow buildings resembling stone-slated and mullion-windowed Cotswold cottages stretched upwards. Apart from the disappearance of the shutters this house at number 13 Holywell has barely changed in the century since Shuffrey painted it. Watercolour 270 x 368mm. OXCMS: 2002.74.14.

Plate 47. Holywell Music Room.
The famous 18th century Music Room looms mysteriously in the background, while the foreground is dominated by the adjacent 17th century house and the autumn foliage of a lush shrub glowing in the murky autumn light. This would have been the view obtained from the right-hand first-floor window of number 51 Holywell, the artist's home between 1906 and 1908. Watercolour. Private collection.

Plate 48. Holywell Street, Bath Place. The three old houses clustering against the old city wall at the southern (far) end of Bath Place (in Shuffrey's composition, the two central houses and the foreshortened one to the right) reputedly relate to the influx of Flemish weavers early in the 17th century. Possibly this suggested to the artist the arrival of his own Huguenot forebears. Not long after the building of these houses, restrictions on the style of new buildings were imposed, so that Bath Place, seen here bathed in the bright sunlight of a summer's morning, remained unique. Probably painted between 1906 and 1908. Watercolour 270 x 367mm. OXCMS:2002.74. 13.

Plate 49. Stable Yard, north side of Holywell Street, 1907. This was formerly the site of the yard and carriage entry of the King's Arms public house. Contemporary buildings have replaced the stable blocks depicted by Shuffrey, on the same alignment (information from John Ashdown). Watercolour 271 x 365mm. OXCMS: 2002.74.7.

Plate 50. The Turf Inn and New College Bell Tower, 1908. The Bell Tower is the only original New College structure to stand outside the line of the old town wall, into the north-east corner of which all the other early College buildings are snugly fitted. The 1908 view captures the juxtaposition of tree-filled college grounds hidden behind stone walls with the tiny oasis of irregular cottages and courts forming the tavern premises, both dominated by a sombre tower. Watercolour 268 x 366mm. OXCMS:2002.74.12.

Plate 51. The Turf Inn, Hall Passage, 1912. Accessible via a low passage from Bath Place off Holywell Street, the tavern is an agglomeration of post-medieval cottages forming irregular courtyards against the old town wall, and can defy depiction; the viewpoint was artfully selected. Watercolour 268 x 365mm. OXCMS: 2002.74.10.

Plate 52. The Turf Inn and New College Bell Tower, 1912. The 1912 depiction, seen from a slightly different viewpoint, also reflects a different mood. Cottage and courtyard life are pursued in the shelter of the ancient creeper-covered town wall and benignly overlooked by a softer-edged Bell Tower shown in paler tones. Watercolour 267 x 368mm. OXCMS:2002.74.11.

Plate 53. Reginald in the Shuffrey studio in Clarendon yard, 1906.

Plate 55. Littlemore Court, St Aldate's, 1914. The growing gap between rich and poor in 19th century Oxford was seen vividly in St Aldate's. Littlemore Hall at number 83, a medieval town house rebuilt and gorgeously decorated in the 17th century, survives as the Restaurant Elizabeth and Alice's Shop. Behind the fine house Edwardian tenants eked a living in the yard served by an open drain; this is now a car park. Watercolour 252 x 345mm. OXCMS:2002.74.47.

Plate 54. Broad Street, Bliss Court. The large properties laid out on the south side of Broad Street in the late 17th and 18th centuries were soon subdivided to accommodate a rapidly rising population living as tenants in 'courts', formerly the back gardens. Just one such court survives in Broad Street, behind number 13, now a service area but retaining the slope down from the old causeway (The name Bliss Court may have been an old memory, as the alleyway had not been known by that name since the 1880s – personal communication from John Ashdown.) Watercolour 255 x 356mm. OXCMS:2002.74.8.

Plate 56

Plate 56, 57. Two Views of Octagon House, Catte Street. The most curious of pre-Reformation Oxford's gate-chapels was the early 16th century free-standing octagonal chapel of St Mary, just north of Smith's Gate at the top of Catte Street. Slighted as a chapel after the Reformation, it was gradually altered for a variety of uses over the centuries. The 20th century rebuilding, as a part of the extension to the north of Hertford College at several dates between 1903 and 1931, has restored it to its conjectured original outward appearance. The south-west viewpoint *(Plate 56)* shows the mellow juxtaposition of the elaborate original Gothic south doorway of the chapel with 18th century plaques and 19th century shop front, while an elevated view from behind *(Plate 57)* reveals the patched stonework, timber additions and chimney-pots of the final phase of mixed tenancies. A timeless, mellow quality has been achieved by showing the east-facing back of the old chapel in morning sunlight, and the south-west front view in the late afternoon. Watercolours. OXCMS:2002.74.5 366 x 268mm *(rear view)*, OXCMS:2002.74.6 268 x 366mm *(front view)*.

Plate 58. St Aldate's, Oxford. The pencil drawing by J.A. Shuffrey shows the St Aldate's frontage of Littlemore Court. Watercolour 355 x 253mm. Private collection.

Plate 59. George Street, 1906. A photograph of the north side of George Street taken about 1900 (*VCH, Oxford IV*, plate opposite 301) locates this shop two doors west of the present Grapes public house, the only pre-20th century building to survive in this stretch of the street. Commercial development began late in George Street, where late 19th and early 20th century shops served the townsfolk. Watercolour 267 x 370mm. OXCMS:2002.74.26.

Plate 60. Grove Place, Black Lion Hall, 1907. Black Lion Hall, now the Kybald Wynchin building, is a surviving example of a stone house of about 1600 built away from the main shopping centre where larger sites were still available. The street itself, formerly Kybald Street, was among others taken over at that period by colleges, and was gated; it remains a quiet backwater close to the city centre. Watercolour 260mm x 360mm. OXCMS:2002.74.31.

Plate 61. The Witches Scene from *Macbeth, played before James I,* from the *Souvenir of The Oxford Historical Pageant, 1907.* Some of the Heads of Colleges are seen centre foreground.

Plates 62, 63, 64. Three of Shuffrey's lantern slides of the 1908 snowstorm: the south side of Broad Street with the Old Ashmolean and Exeter College *(plate 62),* the north side of Broad Street *(Plate 63)* with Trinity College houses and the buildings later replaced by the New Bodleian, and High Street looking west *(Plate 64)* with All Souls College centre background. Private collection.

'Broadway' 1934
St. Margaret 's Road,
Oxford.

James Allen Shuffrey B.W.S.
Reminiscences

I was born on February 25th, 1859, the 5th son of Samuel and Mary Sarah Shuffrey, of Woodgreen, Witney (at that time in the Parish of Hailey). I was registered as James Shuffrey only but being Christened at the end of the year at Holy Trinity Church, Woodgreen the second name of "Allen" was added. I make special note of this, as on occasion it has been found necessary to obtain the Baptismal Certificate. My Godfathers were Dr. Augustine Batt (there is a tablet to his memory in St Mary's Church, Witney) and I have a letter written by him to my mother sending a Christening present of £5 note, and Mr John Allen a cousin of my Mother, whose name was Baylis. His wife Mrs Eleanor Allen was my Godmother and I was named after them. They resided at a large farmhouse, Burmington, near Shipston-on-Stour where I once visited them with my Mother when I was a small boy.

When Mr Allen died, Mrs Allen removed to Broadway where she lived with her sister Miss Taylor until she died in 1913 at 94 years of age. She retained all her faculties and wrote me a nice letter only a few months before. During her latter years it was her wish for me to spend a few days at Broadway each year. She was much interested in my painting and left me a legacy of a few hundreds. I attended her Funeral at Burmington Church.

Huguenots. My ancestor probably came over to England from Flanders as a Blanket Weaver before 1700. He bought the house situated at the top of the Narrow Hill, Woodgreen in 1713 and erected large weaving shops of great height at the back of his house. John Shuffrey was a member of the Witney Blanket Company and he was married in 1720 and the gravestone to his memory is in St Mary's Churchyard. I have a genealogy of all his descendants, mostly obtained from an old bible.

My Grandfather, the youngest of a large family, Samuel by name, went to Chertsey to learn the trade of Tanner and Currier and on inheriting the property probably converted the Blanket weaving shops into a factory for currying leather, and my father who was also a younger son, continued to carry it on very successfully for many years, to which he had added the business of a Tannery. He also farmed about 150 acres of land, mostly arable, about 100 acres of which belonged to my two Aunts, Smith and Williams, both of whom I remember living together on Woodgreen being widows without children.

Both my father and my eldest brother Sam have resided at the old house most of their lives - the old workshops were much out of repair and no longer required for the currying trade which had decayed since the manufacture of machine made boots and shoes. They were pulled down in 1928.

I only propose to enumerate a few events of interest in my memory of my early life and not a family history - my earliest is the Wedding Day of King Edward, then Prince of Wales, in 1863. A procession of children was formed on Woodgreen which I was taken to see and remember quite clearly.

In the summer of 1864 I broke my leg when jumping in the garden of Mrs Clinch on Woodgreen with my playfellows Percy and Marriott Clinch. I remember many details of the illness. A small school for little

Plate 65. James Allen Shuffrey around the time of his second marriage.

Plate 66. Rosa Shuffrey, née Lane.

children was started by Mrs Floyd, living at the bottom of the hill. It started the same Autumn and I was sent, or rather carried there, and had to sit with my leg up on the form.

We were well grounded in English and French. After remaining there for about four years I was sent to a school held in the upper room of the Corn Exchange, kept by Mr Charles Collier (a man with a club foot) who had been Master at the Grammar School, but leaving the Church of England he became a Plymouth Brother and had to leave. His school was very strict and hard worked, only one half holiday a week, and very long home lessons.

Being studiously inclined and unable to play much at games I soon got ahead of the boys of my own age and a curious thing, quite unique, occurred whilst I was being prepared for the Cambridge Local Examination in December 1871. I was taken to Reading with two more boys, it being held there, and on arrival was prevented from sitting for it as I was too young, an extraordinary objection, so had to return home and had to prepare again the next year.

I went to Reading again with another boy named Raikes in December 1872, at the age of thirteen. It occupied most of the week. The result was thought to be very satisfactory – passed with 3rd Class Honours in six subjects - English, Mathematics, Religious Knowledge, Latin, French and Drawing, Flat and Model.

I left school at midsummer after aged fourteen. Much of my pleasure in after life was occasioned by the excellent tuition I received in painting and drawing from Miss Cropper from Oxford, who came one afternoon a week. After a course of Sepia, I had by the age of fourteen a considerable knowledge of watercolours and painted many good pictures (from copy). I was also well grounded in perspective - from which time although employed in other work - I never gave up, during the past sixty years, and this was the only teaching I ever received.

After leaving school it was considered necessary for my health that I should have plenty of fresh air and consequently I became interested in the practical side of farming, gardening and poultry. This continued until the beginning of 1875.

During those years of excellent harvests and good farming prospects my Father then intended me to take it up, having grown strong and learnt most of the practical work of a farm (able to do a good days work) and he then being old found me to be of considerable use. Much of my knowledge I have obtained from an old Shepherd, Panting, who had worked for Father ever since he had been farming (being more of a Bailiff). Father went so far as to make a will leaving me the farming stock etc.

My Mother and others thought I ought to do something better and Leonard having been in London some years as an Architect and married at an early age, it was thought that I might take up some work in which my skill in drawing might be of use. Consequently I went to London in January, 1875, then sixteen years of age, and a possible place found by advertisement for designing work at a business house in Queen's Road Bayswater, but for my purpose there was no prospect and I only stayed a week or two.

Staying on in London I was introduced to several firms such as Benhams Engineering Company, Wigmore Street and others.

Their premium was too high, £300 to £500 for five years. It was almost settled that I should go to an architect, a Mr. Lads in Southampton Row. During these weeks I would start out for the day, with a good map of London and find my way about on foot, visiting the British Museum, The Tower of London, Monument and South Kensington etc. This knowledge attained by finding my way was often of use in later days.

During my absence from home my Mother had been taken ill and in February we were all summoned home to find her lying unconscious, and after three or four days she died on the 25th of February (my own birthday). I then remained at home, nothing settled, and my Father wishing me to do so.

Consequently I took on farming in earnest, until the end of 1876 when a circumstance occurred which changed the whole course of my life. Father invited an Inspector of the London and County Bank, who was then at the Witney Branch, to come to dine with us on the Sunday - and in conversation he found it would be possible for me to get an appointment in the Bank, Father being then an old customer of the Bank, and I being just the right age to make an application to the Head Office. Mr. Hammond gave us the necessary details, and this I was persuaded to do, although not very willingly. My Father's idea was that a few years at Bank work would be good for me, not with the idea of taking it up entirely. This was early in 1877.

I had a favourable reply and was summoned to appear before the Directors, a day which I well remember, going to Lombard Street alone, seeing first Mr. James Gray the Chief Accountant. He took me to the Boardroom, before a lot of old buffers sitting round a large table. I was asked a few questions and especially about my Certificate of the Cambridge Local Examination which I think was then something new, carrying with it an additional £5 per annum salary. Afterwards I was taken to the General Manager, William McKewan.

In due course (on Good Friday) I received a letter of appointment to Oxford Branch. I accordingly presented myself and arranged to commence on the following Monday, April 9th, 1877.

I went to reside at my Uncle's, George Shuffrey, Manor House, New Pembroke Street, but a week after had notice that a vacancy had occurred at Abingdon Branch and was then transferred there. I found there were five clerks and Manager James P. Hammett.

I was taken to lodgings at James Gibbens, the Harnessmaker, Broad Street (Corner of Bath Street) and had a pleasant room at the corner, over his shop and I stayed there some years.

It was a great change to me living alone and providing for myself knowing no-one except the Bank Staff. I made friends of Mark Taylor and C.W. Sewell. I shall not enter into any discussion of Bank life. At first I frequently went home for the weekend, but the train did not arrive back soon enough for business in the morning, so I learned to ride a bicycle, an old wooden "boneshaker". Then I had a bright forty-inch "Coventry" - large wheel in front, small behind, with solid rubber tyres. It required some practice to mount these bicycles and sitting over the front wheel it was well to be prepared to jump off in emergency.

The roads were then macadam, with many loose stones and a large stone, or rut, would cause the rider to pitch head first over the handlebars.

At that date there were very few riders in Abingdon. I was enabled to ride to Witney on Saturday afternoon and back on Sunday eve, or in summer early on Monday morning by breakfast time, starting at 6a.m. Often I would walk back to Abingdon on Sunday evening after tea via Stanton Harcourt and Bablock Hythe Ferry, fifteen miles.

Having been in the Choir of Woodgreen Church, Witney, as a boy and having belonged to a singing class at Witney, I joined the Musical Association at Abingdon (Conductor Frederick Couldrey) having then a high tenor voice. I also sang in the Choir of St. Michael's Church, in the Park, and soon made my "debut" as a singer in the Town Hall Abingdon being vociferously encored on the first occasion. When a boy at home we had taken up theatricals, having a stage in an old workshop, and invited our friends to the performances. Therefore I was soon sought after to join the Abingdon Dramatic Society, which had been in existence some years and some very creditable performances were given in the Town Hall each year. "Frederick Barkins" in "Cool as a Cucumber" was my first debut in an important part. "Plumper" was played by H.J. Brooks - he afterwards became an artist of large groups of figures - Cricket at Lords, House of Commons etc. published by Dickinson and Foster. I met with him again in 1906 when having a picture shown there.

In September 1879 I was very ill with a carbuncle on my chin and throat. After a few days I was taken home in a carriage, and became very ill, the swelling being so great that it was impossible to eat or swallow very little liquid, I was nursed in bed for several weeks by my sister Lizzie, and Mrs Panting at night. The poulticing made much work - after being lanced it got better but I had become so weak and thin that I was unable to return to the Bank for about three months altogether.

1879 was a very wet summer, a disastrous year for farmers, much of the corn was spoilt and some not carried until Christmas - resulting in the bankruptcy of many farmers. I returned to work and remained well for many years.

I was then nearly twenty-one. On my birthday in February, 1880 I received a Legacy of £200 from a division of sale of Aunt Smith's share of the farm. Later in the year I joined the Volunteers, 1st Berks. and we had lectures and examinations of the St. John's Ambulance Association which I found very interesting and passed with a certificate. I also went to camp for three days at Aldermaston Park concluding with an inspection. The rifle shooting was interesting and I did well. In the following year, 1881, the 1st Berks went to the Great Volunteer Review in Windsor Park. The Abingdon Troop left early in the morning by train to Reading and on to Ascot Station from which place we marched to the Windsor Park and the Review Ground, in a broiling hot sun, clad on the first occasion in the new scarlet tunics and helmets and carrying rifles for six or seven miles. The tedious moving up into formation on a very hot day in July was very trying and there were numerous faintings.

We again marched back to Ascot station in the cool of the evening but the entraining of men from long distances first, caused ours to be so late that we did not reach Reading until midnight, and no train left to convey us farther. But we had a very welcome surprise. We were all marched into a large hall at Sutton's Seed stores where a good meat repast was awaiting us, after which we slept on rugs in the factory buildings. Again, we had breakfast there. Afterwards we drilled in the Market Place and returned by train to Abingdon about mid-day. This was the first great Review by H.M. Queen Victoria.

The 18th of January, 1881 was memorable as the date of the Great Snow Storm. After a piercing wind the previous day, Monday, on the Tuesday morning the blizzard commenced. I had arranged to go to a dance at Witney, with Tom Townsend and Ian Rant. We started by the train about 5p.m. then very late. The snow was already deep. Arrived at Radley Junction our train from Oxford did not arrive. The wind was terrific, causing the snow to make deep drifts. After waiting a couple of hours we were informed that no more trains could come. A previous train was snowed up at Kennington. We therefore considered what could be done. I had friends living within half a mile, but it was not thought possible to get there. Knowing there was the Railway Hotel nearby and we met other friends also going to Witney, we went to the Hotel. They said we could have the parlour. A fire was lit there and it smoked furiously at first. We were then requiring a meal not having had anything since mid-day. They had no butter left but could give us fried bacon and tea. The bar was full of people. We adjourned to the room and having our dress coats etc. with us took off some of our wet things and sat round the fire.

After a time a young country girl came with the tea, and as she brought in the dish of fried bacon pitched it over on to the floor, but we eventually got some then settled down round the fire telling tales etc. but gradually some got sleepy and made use of the floor. All communication had stopped with the outside world. When it began to get light we found the snow had stopped so two or three of us thought we would get across to the station by going round drifts. It was not much trouble. An unusual sight awaited us there. The waiting room was crowded with the passengers who had come out of a train - sitting round a big fire, many not knowing where they were - all famished, no food being obtainable. Walking along the platform we came to a long train full of people who had been there all night. The snow had drifted nearly to the top of the train and they did not know where they were. Going back to the Hotel we found it besieged with people trying to get something in the way of refreshments. Seeing there was no possibility of getting any breakfast several of us started to walk back to Abingdon. The road being blocked with drifts we went across the fields in places. We eventually arrived there and let the people know to get supplies of food over there. In the town the men were busy cutting a way along the footpaths. It was still freezing hard so that all traffic was stopped two more days until the Railways could run a train. Five passenger trains were snowed up between Radley and Oxford. I went to the Bank and explained matters, but there was nothing doing. No letters until Friday. Some parts of the canal were swept and we took it in turns to have an hours skating. The ice had been good the previous week and on the Sunday several of us skated to Wantage on the Canal. I got off at Grove and went to friends at Denchworth. Not meeting with the others on my return I skated that night about eight miles alone on a bright moonlight night.

We had never heard of trains being snowed up in Oxfordshire before and certainly never have experienced anything like it since that day, and as I write this in January 1931 it is just half a century ago

The Ball at Witney took place but of course only a small number arrived at the Corn Exchange and on returning home the ladies had to be carried out to the carriages, where they could get them. Several gentlemen from a distance had to be put up for a few days and more dances took place.

When first at Abingdon I joined the Rowing Club and practised in the four-oar, but a sculling boat through the lock to Nuneham and landing at the Cottages on a summer evening was our great delight. The keeper of the Cottages happened to have come from Cogges and knew me and let us land at any time.

Soon in the summer of 1877 I commenced sketching and walked out to a country village with one or other of the bank Staff and made pencil drawings of the Church. These were completed at home and were mounted in a book and the later sketches were made in watercolours. The drawing was mostly correct, but in some cases the foliage was crude. The two albums are still quite good.

In the summer of 1880 I made my first sketching tour. During my holiday I visited my brother Frank then in a business in Eastbourne. Staying a few days I visited Pevensey and Hurstmonceaux Castles. From there I went through Brighton to Southsea and over to Ryde, on the Isle of Wight where I stayed a week at the Crown Hotel, taking long walks to Newport and Cowes, making a good sketch of Carisbrooke Castle en route. Another day to Shanklin with a sketch of the Chine. Then at Eastbourne a sketch of Beachy Head was the best.

During the five years I was at Abingdon Branch it was my duty to go with a cashier to open at East Ilsley on Fair Days through the summer. We started about 9a.m. and drove a four-wheel carriage, going through Steventon and over the Berkshire Downs. At times there were more than 20,000 sheep penned. In fact the whole place seems nothing but sheep pens and Inns - a great amount of business. Sheep were sold in hundreds and penned accordingly by the dealers, many coming from Bedfordshire and distant parts to buy. We were able to go out to a market dinner at the Swan Hotel, full of farmers and dealers. I never enjoyed such mutton to equal it anywhere and also good wholesome plum puddings. Having a good knowledge of farming I always found it interesting to have a chat with the farmers who came in.

In the Spring of 1882 I was moved from Abingdon to Arundel Branch of the London County. At the early part of May I found the country looking very beautiful and the very charming old Castle Park and Town were a great delight. The Bank was in the main street running up the hill to the Castle Gate and I found lodgings in nice rooms over a tailor's shop in the market place.

It seemed as if the place had been selected as the most desirable branch for my artwork, so that I lost no time in making a start at out door watercolour sketching. I soon found several young artists sitting about, working in oil colours, intent on making a living from their work and whilst on any large subject would frequently have to knock off "pot boilers". I soon became acquainted with one or two of them, and often had discussion on sketching - choosing subjects etc., which although working in watercolours myself, were of considerable use to me.

Swanbourne Lake in the park formed a beautiful picture and I sometimes would see four or five artists sitting at work under umbrellas. Commencing on

sketches of a small size the first summer, I made considerable progress, especially with trees, the Park and beech trunks. The river also afforded very attractive bits and I soon took on with about 14" x 10".

My accurate drawing stood me in good stead - so much so that a gentleman visiting nearby, Mr. Levatino, expressed a wish to see what sketches I had made and was very pleased to buy a selection of them (at that time several small ones 10" x 7") This was my first sale and leaving the price to him, he offered me £5 for them, much to my delight. I also had a commission from him to paint an old farmhouse at Lyminster where he was staying.

This being very encouraging I set to work on something larger the next summer and I went out early morning to make a good picture of the town and Castle from the River Arun, in a good light before breakfast. Making a thorough sketch, it was first painted with the shadows in grey and the colours washed on after. This system I had learnt from a very valuable old book by Francis Nicholson (Printed by John Murray 1823). The illustrations were a great aid. I found this way of working to be an immense advantage in starting on a large subject as the above, with much detail. It must be remembered at that time my teaching had solely been from copies at school and other work from Birket Foster pictures. This picture turned out very successful. It was sent with three others, to an Exhibition of the work of Bank men at the Guildhall, London and was especially noticed by the daily papers. I have always appreciated it and it has been hanging in my bedroom for many years. The colours have also remained more permanent for near fifty years than many more recent works.

Plate 67. Rose Lane Grange, 1914. Now called Meadow Cottages, the Grange is seen here from the Botanic Gardens opposite. Shuffrey's *Reminiscences* seem to confirm an association of the place, Rose Lane, with his second marriage, to Rosa Lane; the relationship blossomed in early spring 1908. Unusually for the artist the scene is shown in the very early spring, with a warm south sun casting long shadows against trees just coming into bud. Watercolour 367 x 270mm. OXCMS:2002.74.18.

Plate 68. Buttermere, 1908. The depiction of a landscape in total contrast to southern England shows surprising mastery. Although described by the artist as a 'very realistic sketch', mountains and mist recall the French Impressionists. Watercolour 405 x 279mm. Private collection.

Plate 69. Botley Mill, 1907. Built originally around 1344 along the westernmost branch of the Thames, Botley Mill was one of half a dozen Oxford mills to survive into post-medieval times and may be seen in Oxford maps of the 1870s (information from John Ashdown). The sagging central roofline is suggestive of a medieval timber-framed structure. Watercolour 372 x 271mm. OXCMS:2002.74.54.

Plates 70, 71. Two views of Iffley Mill. The mill is seen still in working condition before the 1908 fire that destroyed it. Both views balance to right and left the Norman tower of St Mary's Church with the poplars between the mill dam and pound lock channels, and above and below, the turgid sky and Thames. Watercolours. OXCMS:2002.74.34 267 x 366mm. *(Plate 71, portrait view);* private collection *(Plate 70, landscape view).*

Plate 72. North Hinksey Church and distant view of Oxford. An old western approach to the city past St Lawrence's church is seen in the rural setting it retained until the building of the Oxford ring road. On the horizon the Oxford skyline gleams under the heights of Headington and Shotover. Close in viewpoint and composition to William Turner of Oxford's *Oxford from Hinksey Hill (see p 28 above).* Watercolour 365 x 268mm. OXCMS:2002.74.55.

Plate 73. Summertown Brickworks. The site of the old claypit and brickworks on the west side of the Woodstock Road is now being developed and was formerly occupied by the company Unipart, the farm and fields to the left by suburban development, and the land to the right by the sports facilities of St Edward's School. But the sun setting over Wytham Hill can still be seen across Oxford Canal (marked by the line of trees) and Port Meadow. The viewpoint adopted is from near the entry to the Unipart and present development site. Watercolour 337 x 245mm. OXCMS:2002.74.52.

Plate 74. Wolvercote. The view of Upper Wolvercote's cottages facing west over Wolvercote Common below St Peter's Church is somewhat more crowded today, but the meadow and pond – now a conservation area – remain. Watercolour 261 x 214mm. OXCMS:2002.74.61.

Plate 75. Godstow, the Trout Inn. The 17th century inn, on the site of a medieval mill, prospers with numerous additions; the rebuild to a closely similar design dates to the Millennium. Only a few stakes of the beautiful footbridge have survived the 20th century. Subtle yellow-green of undergrowth and creepers on the near and far banks of the river alternate with the warm muddy browns of water and sky in broad bands punctuated by the taller trees with their gold to silver early autumn tones. The footbridge invites the viewer to step into the picture – then out again. Watercolour 481 x 304mm. Private collection.

Another large work from a point at the top of Arundel Park is called Turner's bush, with a view of the Castle and sea in the distance - this was on rough paper and direct work - quite good now. It was also exhibited at the same time, 1886.

During the next year I have much enjoyed the visits made to an old gentleman, Mr. Barkshire, formerly in the Duke of Norfolk's Estate Office. He had been quite a capable artist and was very much interested in seeing my sketches, giving me valuable hints. My third and last summer was fairly prolific. I am inclined to think we must have had very warm, fine summers, 1882/85 and that the climate is the best of any part of the kingdom. We took long walks in the beautiful country and frequently on the Downs above.

Plate 76. Shuffrey poses in his studio with his painting of the Trout Inn at Godstow. The choice of this painting suggests he felt it to be one of his masterpieces.

The walk through the park to Whiteways Lodge, and out on to Bury Hill was always a charm. On two or three occasions we walked through Slindon, Halnaker and Boxgrove to Chichester to service at the Cathedral.

Chichester at that time was an interesting city. The cross standing at the centre of four streets is very fine and graceful. The Cathedral is not large, but the precincts, cloisters etc. make for a great charm. The spire had to be rebuilt as the previous one "telescoped" down into the Cathedral in 1854. Boxgrove had an interesting old Priory.

The Bank had a sub-branch at Littlehampton open twice a week and it was frequently my duty to attend there. We drove in a small dogcart, four miles - a very curious arrangement with one clerk from the Private bank "Henty's" who went for the same purpose. One drove there and the other on returning.

We also visited Steyning once a fortnight in the summer. The Manager and one clerk drove over the South Downs, through Findon Gap and under Chanctonbury Ring, starting about 7a.m. as we had our breakfast on our arrival. In bad weather and winter we went by train, via Horsham, where we changed and returned the same way. It made variety. Steyning is very quaint and has a fine old Norman Church. I did not have an opportunity for sketching but have since visited it and made a sketch of the old street, from a spot near which we put up.

There is a fine old church at Arundel, on the top of the Hill, and I was in the Choir most of the time. At that date the church was usually filled and we had a good service. The Organist, Mr. Bartlett, being a friend of mine, I made a sketch of him sitting at the organ and gave it to him which he much appreciated. Curiously when I visited Arundel in 1910 he was still the organist, 25 years after. I have recently heard from him, living with a son at Marlborough.

The Sussex Farmers were a good class and very hospitable. We had frequent invitations to dinner on Sundays to the Heasmans at Calceto, Lyminster, and to John Heasmans at the Manor at Angmering - a fine old mansion, and the Reads of Tarlington. We had a good tennis club and we played on courts lent by the Duke in the Park.

After my third summer I was moved in the Autumn to Petersfield Branch - October, 1884. I had a very enjoyable walk one Good Friday, to Worthing and along the coast to Lancing and walking back to Ford Junction through Rustington. Another occasion to Pulborough.

Petersfield, as I found it in 1884, was a quaint old town with the South Downs a mile or two distant on the South and West, and the hills to the North, with a very picturesque road winding upward through the woods to the higher ground towards Alton. Three miles of really grand scenery - Stonor Hill.

There was a large Bank towering above all the old fashioned houses and shops in the high Street. Being a large market centre with no other market town near, there was much business for a small town. There were about 2,500 inhabitants. My first difficulty was to find desirable lodgings, being somewhat impossible. I settled down in a very old house in Sheep Street - quite a small sitting room looking into a very narrow old street. There was also a Curate who had another room near mine and he was desperately fond of practising classical music for hours together, without any expression.

One of the Bank men named Hemming was a congenial spirit, doing a little painting with considerable skill. He knew all the country around and we had some delightful walks exploring for subjects late the first Autumn. He was also fond of chess and we spent many late evenings as he lived in an old house nearby.

There was a very fine old Church entered from the market place under an old house with an old wheel round window above, and a quaint old Town Hall. I soon joined the Choir. The Rev. J.N. Sumner, Rector of Buriton, was the Vicar and Sir Frederick Currie, Bart. in charge at Petersfield. There was also a good Musical Society doing classical work. My voice, a very high tenor was then at its best and had much practise

- afternoon teas were then just in fashion and generally finished with music and singing - to which I was frequently invited. I distinguished myself in Guardian Angel and Maid of Athens.

I was shortly persuaded by Lady Currie to become the Hon. Secretary of the Church of England Temperance Society and we had a very flourishing branch for some time, having a tea and entertainment with speakers in the Corn Exchange.

The next year a large scheme of drainage was carried out in the town and the C.E.T.S. provided coffee for them before work in the mornings and found a room with curtains under the Town Hall for them to meet in at night, with amusements. It was well attended and much appreciated by the men. The Rev. Wollocomb, then Curate in charge, had a Mission service after Church on Sunday evenings. Mr and Mrs Goble on the Committee were of great service. This was the commencement of a long friendship.

The year 1885 was eventful. Before leaving Abingdon in 1882 I had become engaged to Miss Esther Walker, daughter of Thomas Walker of the Manor House, Denchworth near Wantage, whom I had first met at a dance at Witney in 1880. Spending my holiday there the summer of 1885 it was arranged that we should be married when a home could be obtained and I was able to take one of a builder to be finished by the end of October. I got permission for absence for a few days and the Wedding took place at Denchworth Church, adjoining the Manor on October 31st . I had a carriage and pair from Witney to drive there in the morning. My brother Frank came to be Best Man and Aunt Williams and Mrs Sam Shuffrey went with me.

There was a large family party. We went to London and stayed at the Great Western Hotel a day or two on the way back to Petersfield.

I was then more than 26 years old and my wife Etty, 24. It took us some time to furnish and get the house in order, being new, we named it Laureldean - it was near the station. Having a nice piece of ground I took up gardening. The following year the C.E.T.S. started a Cottagers Flower Show and getting a good many subscribers the Royal Marine Band from Portsmouth was engaged. It was a very wet morning for the show but cleared off fine and we had a large attendance, leaving us with £20 in hand.

The next year it was formed into a Horticultural Show - for all three classes. We had a good schedule and a committee was formed by adding two or three more to the C.E.T.S. Committee. The Vicar, Rev. F.J.E. Caister, was President and I undertook the duties of Hon. secretary. I had been acquainted with the work of the Horticultural Show when a youth at Witney but in Petersfield and district it was something quite new and took some time for the exhibitors to learn how to show.

After the first year or two we had a very large tent from Portsmouth and the number of entries and the competition in the vegetable classes was especially keen. The table decorations were also attractive.

Being so many large houses in the neighbourhood we had beautiful shows of greenhouse plants - not for competition, and one occasion a very valuable collection of orchids. The Marine Artillery - under Winterbotham, and the Royal Marines under Miller generally came. The band, and the presentation of the prizes to all the winners, having a circle round the Bandstand, and a lady of Title to present them was a great feature. Lady Sophia Palmer, Lady Hylton, and Lady Maud Wolmer, I call to mind.

The show continued to increase and we had a fair reserve Fund and an attendance of about 1500 people, but it was seldom a fine day entirely. Then we had two disastrous days. One year a terrific thunderstorm came on about 4 p.m. and lasted an hour or more. Fortunately the large tent held all the people. The next year one of the wettest days I have ever known - day of rain spoilt the attendance. Then the reserve Fund came in useful.

I continued Hon. secretary for seven years until 1893. I was able to win a number of prizes for vegetables and annuals in this amateur class, and on one occasion won the bronze medal of the Royal Horticultural Society for twelve zinnias, open to all. My blooms were the largest I have ever seen and the plants growing three feet high. A large bed of them had been planted where there had been a fowl run.

At the time of my retiring from the post of Hon. Secretary I was presented with a Purse of £20 and an illuminated address with the names of all the subscribers (The account of meeting and presentation is in my press cutting book). I was also elected a Fellow of the Royal Horticultural Society. I continued on the Committee until leaving Petersfield.

There was a very interesting Literary and Debating society which met in the Town Hall weekly during the winter months, and of which I was the Vice President. We had some good speakers and interesting papers read, also some spirited debates. I read an Essay on Art, The origin of honey, Bimetallism, Balance of Trade and other subjects - copy of them in manuscript book. I also led a debate taking Fair Trade versus Free Trade in 1891. The fanaticism of Free Trade was so great at the time, that out of an audience of twenty or more I did not get one vote for Fair Trade. Much that I said at the time would do equally well today, and much that I foretold has been more than fulfilled.

My painting during my twelve years residence in Petersfield was taken up during the summer evenings. I especially remember making paintings of the Heath Pond and distant hills and in the fine summer of the

Queen's Jubilee, 1887, several subjects on the river at Sheet Mill, and Steep Church. Otherwise sketching was too far out to be undertaken in the evenings.

My son Reginald was born on the 1st of September, 1886, at Laureldean, Station Road. After going to a small girls school he went for a time to Churches College. In 1893 we removed to Heath Villa on an elevated position near the Heath and with open views of Butser Hill and Downs. At this house there was an old stable and coach house and we kept some prize bred fowls, taking prizes with an old Cochin cock of great size.

The Queen's Jubilee in 1887 was celebrated by a free tea in a large tent on the Heath and sports in the evening. Mr. Joshua Swan catered and I designed a new mug and cup, with programme of events, which was made for the purpose. The wedding of the Duke of York, now our present King George took place. A meeting had been called to arrange for a celebration, but we had decided not to have one. There seemed to be a number of people at that time not particularly loyal. I was determined therefore that something should be done and Mr Edward Privetts agreed with me so we set about making a collection to give all the children a treat. We soon obtained a sufficient sum to give everyone who wished to come buns and milk, and sports on the heath, preceded by a procession and band through the Town. It was a great success.

I was in good health for many years - upwards of ten years to 1890, without a days absence from work through illness, but in the year that the influenza epidemic began I was almost the first to have it. When I recovered sufficiently I went to work too soon and consequently had not got strong. Then I had another attack the next autumn which was serious and left me weak.

In 1891 we went to Dawlish for a fortnights holiday, for the sea air. I did a little sketching and whilst sitting on the beach at work (my brother Clem has the picture) became known to a Mr. Deverill of Banbury who was staying there for the same purpose. He was a seeds-man and the Founder of the 'Ailsa Craig' onion. He told me he gave ten pounds at a show for some wonderfully good onions and grew from them. His wife and daughter and niece were with him. In 1892, July 15th, Barbara was born. It was the morning after the Parliamentary Election when Mr. Wickham was returned for Petersfield Division of Hants. About this time my brother Leonard and John Read came and stayed a day or two for sketching, and their friends Mr. and Mrs Galworthy Davie who were staying in lodgings near, he doing some sketching too. I have a good water colour of his of the market place at Petersfield as it was then. The houses in front of the church have since been removed so the drawing is valuable.

I have not mentioned that my Father died on February 21st, 1889 in the old Farm House at Woodgreen, Witney where he moved to when my elder brother Sam was married, he living at the old house. He had been suffering for some years. I had been each year to spend Christmas at home and usually part of the holiday. When there I had taken a large photo of him and also of Aunt Williams who outlived him some years. The family, one daughter and six sons all attended the Funeral at Woodgreen Church. It was a very cold day and dull, but I got a good photo of the group, also one with Cousin Harry Shuffrey, of the Bodleian, Oxford.

In 1893 we spent the holiday in Boscombe, taking the nurse girl with us, staying in lodgings in a road not far from Boscombe Pier. Reg was then a boy of seven and Barbara a baby. Unfortunately the baby

Plate 77. Broad Street, 1908. The dramatic quality of the group of 17th century University buildings along the south side of Broad Street is heightened by using the raking sunlight to place them successively in deepening shadow, then lighting the Clarendon's statues of Muses and the Victorian balustrade of classical philosophers' busts from behind. The view recalls the *Oxford Almanack* illustration for 1800, *A View of the Theatre, Printing House & c.*, drawn by Edward Dayes and engraved by James Basire, but the subtly shifted viewpoint creating a path into the composition, and the other dramatic and atmospheric effects are Shuffrey's own. Watercolour 366 x 268mm. OXCMS:2002.74.1.

Plate 78

Plates 78, 79, 80. Three Views of Fisher Row, 1908. The row of humble dwellings leading north from the Castle Mill and Quaking Bridge along the western side of the Castle Mill Stream is thought to have developed after the Civil War. Upper Fisher Row remains as a narrow road, while the middle and most of the southern portions have been redeveloped. Watercolours. *Plate 78. Hythe Bridge and Upper Fisher Row. Houses demolished in 1909.* OXCMS:2002.74.37. *Plate 79. Fisher Row and Castle, 1908.* 379 x 277mm. OXCMS:2002.74.35. *Plate 80. Fisher Row. Houses demolished 1909.* OXCMS:2002.74.36.

Plate 79

Plates 81, 82. Two Views of Oxford Castle and Mill, 1912. One view (*plate 82, below right,* OXCMS:2002.74.39) shows the 11th century tower of Oxford Castle from the north-west at the bottom of Fisher Row, the other (*plate 81, below left.* OXCMS:2002.74.38) from the south-west in Paradise Street. This large establishment straddling the Castle Mill Stream monopolised the town's milling throughout the medieval period. Rebuilt in 1781, it continued in use as a corn-mill until 1929 and was demolished in 1930. The Norman substructure survived until recent excavations. Watercolours.

Plate 80

Plate 81   *Plate 82*

Plate 83. The Plough Inn, 1909. Cornmarket was lined with fine timber-framed houses fronted by shops during medieval and post-medieval times; that at the south-west corner of Cornmarket and St Michael's Street is one of several to survive. Watercolour 268 x 366mm. OXCMS:2002.74.23.

Plate 84. The Lamb and Flag, 1909. The pub occupies a cottage built against the back of the grand St Giles House of 1702. The composition unites two of Shuffrey's artistic enthusiasms, Oxford pubs (of which he painted many), and the recording of buildings in Oxford's old passages. Watercolour 246 x 357mm. OXCMS:2002.74.22.

Plate 85. Magdalen Street, Taphouse's, 1910. The 17th century buildings opposite St Mary Magdalen were mostly altered or demolished between 1867 and 1913 to make way for Elliston & Cavell, the city's leading furnishing store. Taphouse's music shop was the exception, and survived until the early 1970s. Watercolour 268 x 366mm. OXCMS:2002.74.24.

Plate 86. St Cross Road (Holywell Church and Cottage), 1910. The ancient manor of Holywell with the medieval church of St Cross had a village aspect in Shuffrey's time; in the 1960s the modern concrete Law Library replaced the old cottages. Watercolour 368 x 269mm. OXCMS:2002.74.9.

Plate 87. St Ebbe's, corner of Brewer Street, 1912. The spire of Pembroke Hall, background left, and the fragment of old stone retaining wall, foreground right, identify the site of these old houses, a triangular concreted area along St Ebbe's Street, now a car park. Watercolour 269 x 367mm. OXCMS:2002.74.50.

Plate 88. Courtyard in Church Street, St Ebbe's, 1911. Shuffrey found great charm in the city's back alleyways, although half a century earlier a city sanitation inquiry had highlighted the squalid living conditions in alleys and courts off Church Street; most of the street was swept away when the Westgate Centre was built in 1970. (A contemporary map suggests ten possible identifications, of which only the alleyway between numbers 7 and 8 fits – personal communication John Ashdown.) The pencil drawing reveals deep interest in perspective and in details like the irregular roofing tiles. Pencil drawing 195 x 290mm. OXCMS:2002.74.86.

Plate 89. St Giles, old houses at the corner of Alfred Street, now Pusey Street. The houses were demolished in 1912 and the site is now occupied by St Cross College. Watercolour 268 x 367mm. OXCMS:2002.74.21.

had bronchitis, cutting teeth, and gave much trouble which prevented us going about much. I did two or three good sea pictures and took Reg over to Swanage by steamer. We also went by boat to Yarmouth, Isle of Wight. I was not much pleased with it, being low tide. I painted a picture of Yarmouth from the seashore with muddy pools.

Our friends the Gobles, when we went to Heath Villa, went for a time to Southsea, his health being bad, and afterwards bought a charming old house beautifully situated under the Downs at Graffham two or three miles from Selham station on the Midhurst line. We visited them there on two or three occasions and have delightful remembrance of our walks together on the Downs, above Goodwood and also the Church at Lavington. It is in the Park and very small, but in the midst of beautiful scenery. It was the home of the 'Wilberforces' and bought after by Buchanan of Whisky fame.

After my friends death (I being one of his Executors) we were able to sell his house and ground to Buchanan for a good profit. In a house nearby the artist La Thaugue has been residing in recent years. When I retired from the Bank in 1897 the house was to let and we had some thoughts of taking it and being near our friends, but it would have been inconvenient for schools.

In the beginning of 1896 my health began to fail and I had trouble with my eyes which caused continuous headache. I had to consult Mr Hardy the Oculist, requiring several visits and the necessity for wearing glasses always. Still very unwell I was sent for a few weeks to Margate where we resided for the time at Fort Crescent. The weather was very cold but we walked out to the Foreland Lighthouse and to Broadstairs, and Ramsgate. My wife and Reg were

with me and the latter much enjoyed it. Being Easter time we felt the winds too keen, but it braced me up ready for work again. We returned to Petersfield.

I was ill again in the summer with a feverish chill and in bed for a week. I had then been ordered to move to Romford Branch and was allowed a short leave before going. I first went there to see the place and to find a house. My predecessor Mr. Gribble had a nice house in Baster Road, backing on to the Great Eastern Railway at the bottom of the garden, which I afterwards found most objectionable. It was a large branch and my position of cashier made a very long day at the counter. On the Staff was Mr. Kumford whom I had known at Witney, he being in the Bank there when I was at school, but he was apparently become weakly and did ledger work so that I held a higher position. We were good friends and later when I was ill he was very kind, living in the same road. He had a son not much older than Reg.

Not long after our arrival at Romford my brother Albert died very suddenly - it was a great shock to us as he had been over from Gravesend to see us a fortnight before and he had arranged to go for the Sunday again, but a telegram came saying 'very ill and go over' which we did and found that he had died the night before of haemorrhage of the brain. He had had a bicycle accident a month or two before and when last with us had complained of it. The weather at this time had been excessively hot for some time. Whilst at Romford I had been out on good walks to see the country. Upminster was then quite a quiet and pretty old village and on two or three occasions I went to a large market gardener who sent to Covent Garden. I was much interested in seeing large fields of onions, runner beans, vegetable marrows etc.

Whilst living there I was introduced to Mr and Mrs Burleigh Bruhl and spent the evening at their house, at the end of our road. He was then a good artist, but had not risen to fame. I have since met with him in recent years as President of the Old Dudley Art Society.

About the end of September I had been over to Gravesend and coming home across the river at Tilbury possibly took a chill and was very ill on my return. I went to bed and was there dangerously ill for some weeks with a very high temperature etc. After this I had six months leave from the Bank. When well enough I went for a trip to Chester and Southport and then a week at Llandudno, coming back stronger. We afterwards paid visits to our relatives and I stayed at Ealing for a time with Leonard. Returning to Romford I was examined by the Bank Doctor again and he would not pass me for work again so I was called upon to retire on a Pension.

During this time we had left the house with the two children, Reg, about ten years, then at school at Romford, and Barbara, about four, looked after by our old servant Ellen and her cousin with her whilst we were away. Whilst looking out for another home we stayed for a month at Ealing about Easter, 1897, whilst my brother and family were away. We had some thoughts of going to Graffham, in a house near our friends the Gobles, but decided it was too much in the country, and away from our relatives. Leonard happened to have his house at Witney which he had renovated, unoccupied. He said we might go there at a low rent and keep a room for him when he came down.

Thus we packed up again and at considerable expense removed to the 'Old Farmhouse' at Woodgreen. I found the first spring the garden, which is very large, required much work. I was then fairly strong - only my sight was bad, so spent much time in the garden working mornings, and resting in the heat of the day. In the large orchard we kept fowls. Some time later Leonard Junior, my nephew came and resided with us whilst he was superintending the installation of steam wood cutting machinery at their works nearby.

Reg went to the Grammar School and Barbara started at Miss Tarrants. The latter gave my name to Miss Early who was requiring a Master for drawing to her pupils at the Vicarage at Bampton where I accordingly went once a week, generally on my bicycle - teaching three of the Vicar, Rev. Hampshire's daughters, Miss Staples Brown and Miss Hunt. I had been at school with this Miss Early when at Miss Floyds and also a brother had been with me in the Bank at Petersfield.

In the summer of 1898 my nephew Leonard informed me that he was getting married and would want the house we were living in. My brother offered to build another for us in his field on the Woodstock Road and the house was commenced but was not nearly ready by the time we required it. On my way to Bampton I had looked about for houses and found them very cheap. We looked at several and then found that one could be bought for less than £200 with a large garden, well stocked with fruit trees, on more elevated ground on the hill going into Bampton. Seeing that it might easily be much improved by putting in bow windows - the house faced the south and a fine open view over Bampton, we therefore bought it and lived there for four years. We found Bampton a pleasant place to live and were introduced to a number of people by the Vicar's wife. I also found that an old school fellow of mine was a large farmer and ram breeder at Ham Court, formerly part of the Castle, and we became good friends. They were John and Mrs White and our friendship continuing until the death of Mr. White after he had removed to Bath. Dora Esther was born at The Laurels, Bampton on July 3rd, 1900. She frequently went with Barbara to stay at Ham Court and at Coombe Down, Bath in after years.

Whilst at Bampton I did a lot of gardening and bred a number of fowls. I was also persuaded to become Secretary of their Horticultural show. We extended it to agricultural roots and I called on many farmers in the villages round. The show became a great success and was held at the Grange, with a tennis tournament, and attracted a large number of visitors. The cottagers vegetables were remarkably fine. I continued Hon. Secretary for three years.

In the Spring of 1900 I took a chill which developed into rheumatic fever, and after that subsided, gout came on very badly in my feet and hands, being most painful, and being helpless I was in bed for some weeks. I remember being upstairs and having to get out of bed to see the bonfire in Bampton at the Relief of Mafeking.

During the summer of 1902 there were a number of smallpox cases and it continued to spread. They were taken away to a hospital in the forest. Several deaths occurred. The place was quite deserted - no services at Church. We kept away being outside, and it happened that we kept goats at the time which supplied us with enough milk; bread from Brize Norton, and meat from Witney. Just at this time the Coronation of King Edward was to have taken place. It could not have been celebrated at Bampton, but it was postponed.

We left Bampton for Oxford in September 1902. We went to stay at Burnham in Somerset in the Autumn 1899 in lodgings at Mrs Washer. Clem and family were then living at Bridgewater. On one occasion they came over and we were on the sands when Leonard, Pat and boys, staying near also came. I made some good sketches of Burnham on Sea.

During my residence at Bampton I had done a good many water colours of beauty spots near, and the Church and surroundings. In the year 1898 I sent pictures to the Oxford Art Society Exhibition which were hung - and again in 1900 when I was elected a Member.

My exhibits that year contained one of Burnham. Going over to Oxford to spend some time at the Exhibition, when arriving, the Secretary Michael Angelo Mathews, told me that Canon Kennard had enquired about me so he, happening to be there, introduced me to him. The Canon said he had been admiring my work and wished to know whether I was related to Mr. Shuffrey the Dentist in Burnham. Canon Kennard lived in an old collegiate house just opposite Christ Church and asked if I could make a painting of it for him. We went across to look and it was arranged to go over in the Spring. This I accordingly did and made a good large drawing, with Tom Tower above. He gave us lunch. Reg went with me and it took two more visits. He was greatly pleased and had a second one done of it for his brother. He was a Roman Catholic (afterwards Msgr.). He had a good photo made of the picture and sent a number of them round to his R.C. acquaintances. He was a wonderful personality and I often met with him when I was sketching in Oxford in after years. He lived latterly at Burnham and we happened to go down there where notices were up that he was preaching so we went to the R.C. Church and heard him. He was then very old and we read shortly after that he was dead.

The pictures of Burnham having attracted Canon Kennard and the pictures I did for him were thought to be such good work that it was suggested to me by the Vicar that it would be an excellent thing for me to live in Oxford and paint the Colleges. Therefore, when an offer was made by Mr Blyth, son of Canon Blyth, to take 'The Laurels' on lease, we decided to move. Reg had already been living in Oxford to learn of the printing etc. at Aldens. The Oxford Art Exhibition and Canon Kennard meeting me were responsible for the change in my existence, and developing after as The Oxford Artist, especially of the interiors of the Cathedral.

Before leaving Bampton, as I had done a number of interesting pictures and several people wished to see my work, it was thought that an Exhibition of them in the school would be appreciated, so it was arranged for one day - 11a.m. to 5p.m. 3d. each entrance to be given to the vicar for the School fund, and it was quite well patronised. A catalogue was printed and to my surprise quite a number of pictures were sold amounting to more than £20. Another day I took them over to Witney and exhibited at the Corn Exchange upper room, where I had formerly been to school. A fair number of people came but I only sold a few small ones. One of my best pictures was a sketch of some old thatched cottages at Clanfield at a corner of the Church. Strange to say they were all burned down a fortnight after and some elm trees near were removed to widen the road. I also painted the Horde Chapel and Cote House for a descendant of the family from America visiting the old country.

In September we packed up again, selling off the fowls and moved to Thorncliff Road, Oxford. I soon started my artwork and have a large watercolour from near the Martyr's Memorial, of the St Giles front of Balliol with the autumnal hues on the creeper. It was exhibited at the Oxford Art Society and also used for a postcard. I worked on the Colleges and Cathedral and they were selected by Ryman 'Picture Dealers', High St. and shown in their window - (also Court Cole, Broad St.). I also commenced with a drawing class and soon got several pupils. We went out sketching in the summer months and also went over to Abingdon occasionally for the same purpose.

Whilst at Bampton I commenced riding a tricycle and found it more useful for carrying my sketching easel etc. so that I was able to visit the places round Oxford. The lessons continued and after a time I took a room at 6 High Street near Carfax to save bringing my sketching work back as then I was doing some large pictures of the Colleges. Later there being another room vacant I had a show of pictures to take friends in to see them. At this time I was also painting the interior of Christ Church Cathedral, a new work for me but one which brought me into notice (but of no profit as they would not sell). Here I met with Miss Anson of All Souls and she arranged for me to teach two of her nieces at All Souls - later Mr F.A. Anson returned from New Zealand to live at Stanton Harcourt and I went there a few times each year for the day to take a sketching class of his four daughters (with sometimes a friend staying) going by train to Eynsham station where I was met with a carriage. The beautiful grounds of the Lodge with Pope's Tower, the Church and moat, made an ideal spot for many sketches but somewhat too difficult for my pupils. I generally had lunch there and was driven back to Eynsham.

In the year 1903 I was invited by Canon Arthur Shuffrey to visit him at Arncliffe Vicarage, Yorkshire and paint his Church and other views, going there via York where I stayed the night and was charmed with the old streets, making a good picture of 'The Shambles'. Arncliffe is beautifully situated in a deep valley with a stream flowing over boulders, and the Church standing on the banks is a charming subject. A drive of four miles up a narrow lane most of the way, brought my cousin and I in a little pony cart to Halton Gill where he held a service on Sunday afternoons. A very small Church joining the school is attended by farmers from the outlying farms and I was greatly surprised at the musical service, full choral.

On another occasion we walked up the mountains to call on farmers, parishioners in the valley. When in view of Pen-y-ghent I was able to make a good sketch of it - but it rains in that mountainous district and soon a storm came over. When I had made my drawing I took shelter under rocks. I waited hoping to finish my sketch in watercolour but hurriedly I had thrown all my water away. It bethought me to catch some water off my umbrella, which soon filled my dipper and I was able to complete my picture, also another rapid sketch, with sunshine after shower.

The rain came on later and we were drenched on returning to Arncliffe. At that time this place was only reached by a bus from Grassington station, via Skipton, whilst now 1931, it can be reached from Oxford in the day, in fact the Canon, although suffering from Rheumatoid Arthritis has been able to be driven up there by his son in the day and has gone several years to do duty - this past year, 1930, he was too much of a cripple. He has written several books called 'The Craven Worthies'. But this is a digression.

I also visited Broadway to see my very old Godmother, Mrs Allen, and generally stayed a few days at Mr Davis's on the Green. He was Fac-to-tum for the old lady and had a small farm, using her meadow for his sheep. I had an opportunity of taking some good photos of him with his sheep in the meadow. I always did sketching if fine and one occasion made a really charming view of the hill from Lord Lifford's garden. I also met an old gentleman, Captain Treherne, who was a great collector of old paintings and he very much appreciated my work so gave me a commission to paint two or three. Mrs Ruth Jackson also required a painting of the garden front of her house at Broadway. This gave great satisfaction.

About 1904 the coloured postcard came into fashion and Mr R. Peel was publishing a number of Oxford views made from drawings by the local artists and he came to me for six pictures of the Burne Jones windows in Christ Church to be reproduced in colour - which I accordingly did. Then Alden & Co. published a set of six called 'The garden series of the colleges'. Next Faulkner & Co. of London had six Colleges to reproduce as a set which became very popular - after that I had a set of six printed from my best large pictures of Oxford (first by Mowbray & Co. Ltd.). The Cathedral sets were used in a book of Oxford views published by R. Peel.

About this time my brother Clem was staying on the Wye at Symond's Yat and much struck with scenery there he asked me to go there, which I did taking Barbara with me. It was a week of very beautiful weather and I was fortunate in getting lodgings at the Station Master's house (Mr. Parry). It was near, and overlooking the Wye. I did some large pictures from near the station and of the Seven Sister Rocks. The walks through the woods were very beautiful. I went up to the Rocking Stone, and to Goodrich

Castle and to Church on Sunday at Whitchurch by boat. Also to Ross and Monmouth and spent another day at Tintern Abbey making a large watercolour from the hill.

After leaving Petersfield we had kept up acquaintance with Mr Arthur F. Jones who had built himself a good substantial house, from his own plans, on the side of Cranleigh common overlooking the Windmill, then a very picturesque feature of the view from his house. I stayed with him frequently in the Autumn to get the tints of the beautiful Surrey common.

My friend had taken up photography when at Petersfield and as I had previously done so myself was able to put him in the way of it. He spared no expense using a whole plate camera. At one time we used to hire a waggonette and take long drives, especially out towards Selborne (taking my wife and children) and with our cameras recording the most interesting and picturesque views we could find. Mr. Jones printed all these in platinotype and when he had completed a good number, the best, especially of old cottages were carefully arranged in large books with catalogues.

He continued doing this in Surrey so that when I visited him, being a good walker, he was able to guide me to the best subjects for painting, and Smithwood common made numerous pictures but a view in Autumn from Winterfold Heath - looking South over the valley was my favourite. There were several old homesteads and barns. These when visited later had been modernised for private houses and the owners had purchased my pictures of them.

Ewhurst was very charming. I have one autumnal one rich in colour showing the Church spire. We also drove through Albury by the silent pool to Shere, at that time a quiet little place, and stayed some hours dining at the old Inn. There were four or five artists sitting round sketching and I made a small sketch looking down the village.

On one occasion when staying at Cranleigh I went with my friend to an outing of the Guildford Field Club to visit the grave of H.M. Stanley at Pirbright Churchyard. The monument consists of one immense slab of granite, roughly hewn, about eight feet high. A poem, specially written for the occasion was recited at the grave, during which I made a rough drawing of the Gravestone. We afterwards visited the home of Lady Stanley and the Museum in the grounds containing relics of Stanley, everything being left as at his death. We all had tea there, afterwards walking round the grounds.

When Mr. Jones visited us at Oxford in 1904 - July - he came from Kingston by the Thames steamer. He always preferred it to the train. It rained almost continuously on his journey and we had a very wet time, so that when he wished to return the river was so high that the steamers could not run, not being able to go under the bridges.

My health had greatly benefitted by the open air life at Witney and Bampton and my sight improved, but I could do little reading for some time as my memory failed and I could not recall what I had been reading. In the middle of 1900 - about March, I got a chill and rheumatic fever as mentioned before and many people said that Oxford would be the worst place for rheumatism, but I am pleased and thankful to record that I did not suffer in that way although I was continuously sitting about sketching in all sorts of weather - for the past thirty years. My wife who had developed asthma when at Petersfield, having inherited it from her father, continued to suffer with it and more so when combined with bronchitis at Bampton, when staying away at Radley having let the Laurels to the Farmers. She was very seriously ill with pneumonia when at her brother's which left her more weak. This was 1901 - went to Oxford in 1902 and she was fairly well but in the autumn of 1905, the severe winds in October brought on acute bronchitis and she passed away on the 25th October through heart failure. She was buried at Woodgreen Church, Witney.

We continued to live in Thorncliff Road until the following March. My lease having expired, Reg finding it a long way for his work and Barbara at school, aged thirteen - in the City would be more convenient and save my walking to and fro to the colleges for painting. We were able to obtain a small house, No 51 Holywell St. There was one large room, north aspect, which was admirable for work. In the previous October, when my wife was so ill, I had been asked by Mrs Whitmarsh to have a show of my pictures at a large Bazaar and Meeting of the Home Missions, and had a stand in the front of the platform in the Town Hall allotted to me. Unfortunately I was only able to be there a part of the time and Mr Mardon Mowbray very kindly attended to it for me. This was my first public show of pictures in Oxford. For a few years afterwards I had a small show in the Assembly Rooms, Town Hall, at the Arts and Crafts Exhibition - commencing in 1906.

This was also a memorable time with the General Election in January of that year, when the Conservatives took up Tariff Reform, brought about by Joseph Chamberlain. I had studied this question for years and was greatly in favour of it. My friend Councillor Sidney Scott, Chairman at Summertown Conservative Committee rooms prevailed upon me to join them and I went out canvassing in that part. The Conservatives had been hanging on for some time and Balfour by his undecided policy was very much out of favour. There was a very noisy meeting in the Town Hall on the night before the Election. 'The big and Little Loaf' and Chinese Slavery in South Africa was the cry of the Liberals. Lord Valentin could hardly get a hearing. The meeting had nearly come to an end when a big burly Parson (Rev. Stevenson) with stentorian tones, held the peoples' attention, exposing the Liberal lies, he himself having been a Chaplain in South Africa. The opinion of the meeting seemed to change but Lord Valentin only had a hundred majority. The Conservatives lost seats in all parts, Balfour himself being beaten. I joined the Gordon Habitation of the Primrose League later in the year.

In 1906 we left Thorncliff Road at Lady Day and moved to 51 Holywell St., one of the old houses belonging to Merton College. It was very handy for the College gardens for sketching and I spent much time about New College with the old Cloisters and Bell Tower (used by Cromwell for stabling their horses) the old City Wall too, and from a balcony at the top of the house I made a rather unique sketch of the old roofs, Bell Tower and the west end of New College.

About this time I was doing very large pictures of the Colleges. All Souls, Brasenose, Magdalen, Merton, Christ Church and Wadham, St Mary's- the-Virgin Porch, the High Street and The Turl besides many of the old houses in Holywell and other parts, many of which have since been demolished. My time then was almost entirely devoted to my work and I did not leave Oxford for many days. In bad weather much time was spent at subjects in the Cathedral. The large picture of the nave, The Latin Chapel etc. with smaller ones, six of which were reproduced as postcards, making twelve in all - none of these have ever found purchasers although so much admired.

During the summer I went to London to the Academy and galleries looking in at small shows in Bond Street, one at Dickinson and Forster. There I enquired about having a show and they offered me what appeared fairly reasonable terms and later I determined to hold a show of my Oxford pictures etc. This took place at the end of September but being so fine the attendance was very small and at that time I was personally known to so few about Town. There were some good press reports - about seventy pictures were shown and only a few sold and something would have to be done with the fifty or sixty framed pictures.

Several old friends whom I had not seen for years met me at the Show. H Jarmyn Brooks, whom I had known at Abingdon in theatricals about twenty five years before was then at Dickinsons, making large paintings of Cricket at Lords in a room there, and people came for him to put their portraits in the picture. Large prints were sold made from several of his works. I also found that he had been employed by Queen Victoria to restore her paintings, for many years.

At this time Reg was about twenty and at home with us spending his time doing specimen drawing for advertisements. He had already done some small headings for the Isis varsity paper. We looked about for a possible room for a Studio and at last came across a loft with good top and side lights, entered up stairs from the yard of the Clarendon Hotel. With white-wash and paint we made quite a good place of it and took a three year lease at £20 a year.

My pictures from London were sent down and hung up making quite a good show, and fortunately meeting with a suitable table and large turkey carpet in a furniture shop in Witney (looking in for something to do having missed my train) I bought both for old 50/-. The carpet has been a good old servant in continual wear - looks quite as good now, twenty years after. Reg had a good place for his work and at the same time looked after the pictures when people called to see, as in the Summer and Autumn we had a large bill hung on the Clarendon Gates, announcing the Private View and at times we had quite a number of visitors - a great many Americans and foreigners.

Rev J.W. Tudsbury came to the Studio requiring maps of Wirrall, Cheshire in the time of the Danes to illustrate the sites of battles and he became a frequent visitor. In 1907 I accompanied him to Chester and various parts of Wirrall to make sketches for the illustrations of his book. Unfortunately he died before it was published. He was a very staunch friend, but very eccentric. The description of our sketching tours together in Cheshire, also in Nalines, Bruges and Treves are in the series.

During the winter the Rev May of Christ Church was in charge of Holywell Church. He got up a theatrical entertainment in the Holywell Music Room for funds in aid of Choir funds. Reg and I with a number of friends took part - 1907 was the great Oxford Pageant held in the meadow at the bottom of Broad Walk, near Magdalen Bridge. A large stand was built for seats for the visitors, and bridges across the Cherwell. There was much rain and the Pageant ground became flooded. I took part as a Head of College in the James, the 2nd episode; Barbara, a lady in Elizabeth, and Reg two or three scenes.

Plate 90. St Giles Church and cottages, 1914. The island of buildings around the medieval church, of which only the tower is seen, glows in a blaze of golden autumn foliage, while over to the right a child makes a purchase from a higgler's pushcart. The proliferation of traffic control measures since Shuffrey's time have transformed the scene without altering the buildings. Watercolour 367 x 267mm. OXCMS:2002.74.20.

Plate 91. Broad Street, Old Clarendon Building, 1915. Shuffrey may have adapted the viewpoint used by William Monk in his etching, 'The Broad looking West', which was used for the Oxford Almanack for 1905. The Clarendon Building, dominated by Thornhill's statues of the Muses, is combined with pale filtered sunlight and huddled passers-by to create a rather sombre image of wartime Oxford. The impressionistic treatment of Broad Street's shops and college buildings winding westward is also notable. Watercolour 381 x 271mm. OXCMS:2002.74.2.

Plate 92. Thame, 1920. An early sports car is shown centrally. Watercolour 375 x 279 mm. Private collection.

Plate 93. River scene, Cherwell, 1923. Probably painted north of Summertown near where the ring road is carried over the Cherwell. Watercolour 336 x 254mm. Private collection.

Plate 94. Clifton Hampden, bridges and Barley Mow, 1928. The banked clouds elevate and add interest to the top of the composition, as do the closely observed details of the riverbank to the bottom. Watercolour 368 x 266mm. Private collection.

Plate 95. Waterstock, 1930. One of the latest-dated pictures by the artist, painted at the age of seventy-four. Watercolour 368 x 247mm. Private collection.

Plate 96. Chalgrove. Shuffrey highlights the village's most notable feature, the watercourses on either side of the principal road with access to the houses by footbridge. Watercolour 375 x 279mm. Private collection.

Plate 97. Old Cottages at Radley, 1914. The ancient timber-framed structure of the foreground cottage is shown in sympathetic detail, while the further cottage seems to bob in the misty field like a ship at sea. The economical use of the verge for growing cabbages has been spotted by an experienced gardener. Watercolour 368 x 266mm. Private collection.

Plates 98, 99. Two Views of *The George Hotel yard, Dorchester, Oxon, 1926.* The two views painted of the same subject in the same year from nearly the same viewpoint illustrate the artistic licence Shuffrey sometimes took in the depiction of foliage and shrubs. Watercolours. 348 x 267mm (with chickens on the left). 336 x 267mm (chickens on right). Private collection.

Plate 99

Plate 100. Clifton Hampden, 1928. Shuffrey's paintings of Oxfordshire villages in the 1920s show views and buildings that have changed very little, in contrast to many of his pictures of Oxford. Watercolour. Private collection.

Plate 101. Dorchester, Oxon, 1926. Watercolour. Private collection.

Plate 102. Almshouses, Ewelme. Although the courtyard is empty of human figures, the little pump and trough recall a personal aspect of social life in the antique apartments. Watercolour 368 x 279mm. Private collection.

Plate 103. Summerfields School. The school's playing fields stretch south along the Cherwell, dominating the Victorian, Edwardian and later main school buildings seen at centre right. The composition is eccentric but successful in balancing the clustered buildings with the open sky and fields, reflecting a certain sympathy with the viewpoint of the school's inmates, and demonstrates Shuffrey's skill in dealing with an uninspiring immediate foreground. Watercolour. Private collection (Summerfields School).

Plate 104. Blackhall Farm, 1924. This is one of two or three 18th century farm buildings to survive amid the suburban development of 19th and 20th century Summertown. With later additions, it stands on a corner plot now formed by Charlbury and Garston Roads. The pencil study shows a farmhouse built up against a classic 18th or 19th century hay barn, and is masterful in indicating structural details, light and shadow, and foliage, without the aid of colour. Pencil drawing 320 x 228mm. OXCMS:2002.74.63.

Plate 105. Christ Church, 1927. Details of Littlemore Hall on the far left and the Cathedral far right are delicately sketched. The old houses on the right, which have made way for the building housing the University Music Faculty, are highlighted. Pencil sketch 271 x 371mm. OXCMS:2002.74.67.

J. Allen Shuffrey
1927

Ch. Ch. Oxford
1927

Beam Hall

Plate 106. Merton Street, Beam Hall. Pencil drawing 210 x 295mm. OXCMS:2002.74.80.

Bp. King's Palace
OXFORD
Dated 1628.

J. Allen Shuffrey

Plate 107. Bishop King's Palace, Oxford. The Old Palace at numbers 96-97 St Aldates was originally two separate Tudor houses. Pencil drawing. Private collection.

The Castle Mill
OXFORD

J. Allen Shuffrey

Plate 108. The Castle Mill, Oxford. This detailed study is interesting in showing the earthen embankment behind St George's Tower. The bare branches of the trees indicate that the sketch was made in wintertime. Pencil drawing. Private collection.

I made an Autumnal visit to Mr Jones at Cranleigh and did some good pictures of the Common, also to Broadway for a day or two in the Spring. In the Autumn of 1907 Reg, who had been getting a folio of his advertisement designs and was now become more accomplished, went to London and joined some other young fellows after a time doing the advertisements for Spiers and Ponds etc.

I kept the Studio in Clarendon Yard until the lease expired at Michaelmas 1908. In the Spring I had an Exhibition of my pictures there and sent out a number of cards of invitation getting quite a number of visitors. I have not previously mentioned that in 1907 we started a book for visitors to sign their names. I had sent an invitation to Miss Cross, Winchester Road, but she was going abroad and gave the card to Miss Lane (who was keeping house for her). She visited my show about March, on one or two occasions and with Miss Cross at Easter.

About this time, April 24th 1908, there was an extraordinary fall of snow, eighteen inches deep. The streets were blocked with snow stopping the traffic. The Varsity men were just 'coming up' and had great difficulty to get their luggage from the stations. Being a Saturday market the farmers and carriers could not get home. It stopped snowing in the evening and we cut out a footpath in front of our house, then at 51 Holywell. On the Sunday morning the sun shone brightly and the streets were almost impassable with slush and water. Taking my camera I made several snapshots in the streets. Some photos were afterwards made into lantern slides. I also started to make a large watercolour. Being deep with snow and trees in leaf at the same time was unique.

After the snow came the flood. The snow melting so quickly caused the floods to be very high at Oxford. Being such beautiful weather I started out with my paints on Thursday evening, April 30th and made a picture from Magdalen Bridge looking towards St. Clements Church, and the meadow one sea of water. Afterwards I went into Christ Church meadow and was making a sketch of Christ Church and Merton with Merton field under water. Whilst painting there Miss Lane came along with the intention of going round the meadow. I was just leaving to go to a Primrose League Meeting in which she was much interested.

The next morning, May 1st, I went as usual when living so near to hear the singing on Magdalen Tower at 5a.m. and met Miss Lane there, standing at the entrance of Rose Lane.

Meeting on several occasions and at the house of our mutual friend Mrs Badcock we agreed to get married and as I was leaving the house in Holywell (through building operations) circumstances favoured an early marriage. Looking at various houses we found 99 Woodstock Road belonging to my old friend Ryman Hall. The Wedding was fixed for July 2nd, 1908 at the house of Colonel Foster of Berkhamsted. I went to Berkhamsted on July 1st and stayed the night at the King's Arms Hotel. Reg came down from London and was Best Man and Leonard came over from Ealing. The Wedding took place in the morning - Colonel Foster had a number of the Lane family to the breakfast.

It was very hot, fine weather when my wife and I started from Berkhamsted by L. & N.W. Railway to Penrith on a tour of the English Lakes. We were commencing with Ullswater so having spent the night on the way we went by the coach to Pooley bridge (six miles) there joining the steamer which goes up the Lake. The lower reach bounded by low hills and woods are not distinctive of Lakeland, but rounding the Hallin Fell we are in the middle reach and Helvellyn and other Fells rise continuously from the edge of the Lake, and we become enveloped in grandeur. After rounding Birk Fell the view enhances and the Lake appears to wind into the recesses of the mountains, and with peaks of the Helvellyn range it stirs the imagination. Soon the grandeur of the Lake reaches its climax and we enter the upper reach with Glenridding and Patterdale coming in view. Near the Hotel of that name is the landing stage, and in a few minutes we are in this most picturesque little village in quest of 'Hotel Accomodation' which being so limited we almost despair, but on taking lunch at the only restaurant we find it possible to secure a bedroom there at Rose Cottage. We returned to Penrith to fetch our luggage and spent the evening looking round the old town, taking a second trip up the Lake next day when it seemed even more beautiful. We stayed several days and being fine weather made a large sketch of Lake Ullswater and another large picture of the river rushing down to the lake, with the Helvellyn range in the distance. Skybarrow Crag is the subject of another.

We walked out to service at Patterdale Church, prettily situated, having a most enjoyable time in what I still consider the most beautiful of the Lakes. Leaving Patterdale by coach we arrived in Keswick, the most important town in Lakeland, and we were fortunate in securing rooms for a week at Lane Rigg, overlooking the mountains and Derwentwater. Keswick is a good centre, an old town, some quaint corners especially an inn yard, with old cottages and mountains behind forming a good watercolour subject.

My most important picture was from the Head of Derwentwater with the Lake and the island with Cat Bells. Another from Castle Head takes in the whole of the Lake with Borrowdale in the distance.

About two miles on the road to Borrowdale we climbed a path for half a mile and reached Ashness Bridge, a rude erection over a mountain stream. Seen by evening light, over the trees on the right one sees half the Lake and Keswick on the left, with Skiddaw towering above in the distance - this made a charming subject.

Continuing the road to Borrowdale we pass the Falls of Lodore, a secluded cascade at times, with lovely surroundings. After a long period of dry weather the Falls had become only a trickle of water but I made a sketch, somewhat interesting. At 4 miles is Grange Bridge over the Derwent. Looking up towards Borrowdale forms a good picture.

On Sunday we visited Crosthwaite Church - half a mile. The parent Church was said to have been founded there in 553, but the present Church a thousand years later. Southey's grave is in the Churchyard. The Bridge over the Greta river is on our way, near which are the pencil factories.

Keswick has long been famous for its black lead pencils. We bought some with one's name printed on them if desired. Another day we went by the coach to Buttermere through the most beautiful scenery and especially the Honister Pass, arriving at Buttermere. Lunch at the Hotel and during the short stay I was able to make a very realistic sketch of Buttermere just after a shower with the mist hanging on the mountains.

Having spent a week in Keswick we took the Coach to Windermere passing Thirlmere Lake, Grasmere and Rydal Water. The old Church at Grasmere was most interesting and I should much like to have had an opportunity of sketching the interior. At length we reached Ambleside. The only thing to attract my attention was a quaint old house built on the top of a bridge over a ravine, with a small stream and boulders, on the side of the main road. I stayed here for sufficient time to make a fair sketch of it. By the time we reached Windermere a heavy rain had settled in but I had time to make a rapid sketch of that end of the lake and the range of mountains. Our steamer trip to Bowness was under cover and little could be seen. Glad to get in shelter we booked for the night at the Old England hotel close to the lake - very expensive.

The next morning we made our return journey staying to visit my brother Frank at Walsall en route.

I now propose to write the various sketching tours, a different one for about 20 years.

1908   The English Lakes.
1909   Berkhamsted, Hemel Hempstead etc.
1910   North Devon, Minehead to Clovelly.
1911   Barmouth, Dolgelly. Belgium and Treves.
1912   Hastings, Rye and Winchelsea Canterbury, Chester and Shrewsbury.
1913   Whitby and coast towns. Durham and Richmond.
1914   The Rhine. Cologne, Coblenz, Remage Rhens, Boppard, Caub, Goarhausen, Oberwessel, Baccharach, returning to Amsterdam when war began.
1915   Burnham, Glastonbury, Bristol, Wye Valley and Chepstow.
1916   Hinton Parva, Berkshire Downs, Quainton
1917   Chepstow, Bristol, Wye Valley, Hereford and Ross.
1918   Looe and Polperro and Fowey.

1919   North Wales, Harlech, Criccieth, Bedgelert etc.
1920   Tenby, Saundersfort, Lydsty Manor and Pembroke.
1921   Seaton, Lyme Regis, Dorchester, Frome etc.
1922   Edinburgh, Stirling, Callender and Trossachs, Dunbar, Berwick, Alnwick.
1923   St. Ives, Falmouth etc. Totnes and Bath.
1924   King's Lynn, Hunstanton, Blakeney and Cley. Norwich etc.
1925   Bury St. Edmunds, Walberswick and Southwold.
1926   Sea View, Isle of Wight. Burnham, Lynmouth, Ilfracombe.
1927   Bournemouth, Salcombe and Mevagissy.
1928   Ventnor, Isle of Wight. Gadshill, Hunstanton, Lincoln and Peterborough.
1929   Saracens, Woking, Witley, Taunton, Wiveliscombe.
1930   Saracens, Godalming and Charterhouse, Windsor and Eaton.
1931   Torquay, Totnes and Bath.
1932   Sidmouth and Exeter.
1933   Port Isaac, Padstow.
1934   Worthing, Bramber etc.
1935   Ludlow, Bridgnorth and Sidmouth.
1936   Weymouth.

Art Society

Elected a member in 1900 - I have continued to show the full number of works and except for space they have all been hung. Was elected on the Committee and made Hon. Secretary in 1922 receiving the notice of election to that post when staying at Callender on my Scotch Tour - Matthew Webb having resigned through ill-health. Social evenings were held in the Holywell Music room. The members were entertained to tea at the Randolph Hotel after the Private View in 1930 to commemorate the 40th Exhibition. The members, over forty in number were received by Mr New and myself and we spoke afterwards. The reports of the shows each year, and my exhibits are in my 'press' book, also catalogues.

I was an Exhibitor at Reading, Cheltenham, Worcester and other shows. I also commenced to show at the Old Dudley Art Society, London and was elected a member. A good picture I made of Looe, Cornwall was sold there.

The British Water Colour Society was founded by Paul Brinson and I was elected a member, a first, and have continued to send pictures to their Exhibitions held in various parts of the country.

In 1912, I was asked by Dr Williams of Summerfield School to teach a class of about fifteen boys, for an hour, twice a week. I commenced in May that year and continued until 1930 - the boys were very high class, several with titles. I taught them model drawing and sepia. The best one, Pasmore, went to Harrow and soon became head of school in drawing, taking the special prize for three years. Another, named Merton, went to Eton and distinguished himself, getting head boy in Art - some of his portraits were reproduced in the Eton Journal (four masters of the school). Pasmore continued after leaving Harrow and sent to our Oxford Art Exhibition, being made a member. He also got a picture hung in the Academy, and sold, when about twenty years old.

Reginald exhibited sketches at the Art Society in 1908/09. Barbara had a picture hung in 1909/10. Dora made a sketch at Blakeney which was hung at the Art Society the same year and the President proposed her for membership in 1924.

In many respects the 'times' were very different when I was a boy, from today 1931. Young people at that time had to make their own amusements whilst today in towns they have the Cinema, Theatres, Cafes and endless amusements, by paying for them.

Cigarettes and tobacconist shops had not started. few kinds of tobacco were sold at the grocers. My father generally smoked a long wooden pipe, or the long clay called the Church warden, which was in general use indoors. Spittoons - a round iron platter filled with sawdust, as everyone smoking required to spit. Number of people together had several spittoons. I used to have to fetch Father's tobacco when I was quite small. *2oz of Best Birdcage tobacco please*", price 8d or 9d the packet. Snuff was usual amongst old people and they had pet snuff boxes. I did not smoke at all until I was about thirty five and then tried a pipe which did not succeed. Cigarettes, I first remember, unless one made them by hand, were Ogden's Guinea Gold and Gold Flake in yellow tins - about 1895.

Ladies made afternoon calls on their friends 3 to 4 o'clock and would be offered wine, port or sherry, or poorer houses ginger wine. Tea was usually 5p.m. and friends were specially invited to come to spend the evening, generally, having supper about 8p.m. home made cakes at tea, or crumpets and toast. No bought or fancy small cakes. A party of young and old people sat round a large table and played round games at cards, using ivory counters at about 1d a dozen. Loo, Nap, Speculation, Pope Ivan, played with a special board for the counters, were usual, and draughts and Chess. Whist was always played by old people and as a boy I used to have to play very frequently with Father and two old Aunts who lived near. They were very particular about playing correctly and not talking. We used to play 1d a game.

The game was Ten and honours counted one old penny.

Many families had a piano and singing, when everyone had to take their part. When quite a small boy I used to have to recite or sing to the company. My mother would accompany me. One song I sang was 'Slap Bang here we are again'. In those days there seemed always a popular song going, which boys whistled and sang about the streets until another new one came out.

The Feast or Fair at Witney was looked forward to by everyone, the second week in September. It was very large, covering the whole of Church Green and the Market Place etc. It used to last all the week until it was limited to three days. It was much more interesting in those days. Childrens' toys were nearly all bought at the Fair. Long rows of stalls forming an arcade sold dolls, toys and ornaments, all set out on them.

Then the shooting gallery and roundabouts, mostly turned by hand, afterwards by steam, with horses and an organ - variety of shows, with people dancing on a platform in front. Then there was Norlands Theatre which had a large tent and dancing outside until the performances began about 8p.m. - once nightly. It stayed a fortnight. The piece I especially remember was East Lynn - usually serious pieces.

Large circuses came at other times on to the Green and had a procession all round the town. I learned to dance when at school - country dances, quadrilles, Sir Roger de Coverly and Polkas. After, grown up Lancers, Caledonians, Waltz and Schottisch. There was a large dance or Ball in the Corn Exchange every January, attended by about 200. Also a Twelfth Night party for old and young, beginning with tea and

entertainments until 8p.m. when the children left and the older ones stayed on to dance. About 400 went and this has been kept up. There was a good Flower Show held in August, with the Grenadier Guards Band, conducted by Dan Godfrey, quite a first class affair - we exhibited there a little.

Then the Witney Athletics sports started when I was a boy, held always on Easter Monday, down in some meadows, but later in our close, at the back of the Farmyard, and we used to have one of our wagons to sit in and get a good view. Leonard, I remember, running in the half mile race, falling down within a few yards of the winning post, having been in the lead. On another occasion Clem went in for the Pole jump and walking race but I don't think he won. My older brothers Sam, Albert, Leonard and Clem, were all much older than me, there being a gap of nearly five years between Clem and myself and Frank two years younger.

There were two families of Clinch. Our greatest friend Charles Clinch, a Brewer who lived on Woodgreen and had four sons, and John Marriott Clinch, a Miller who lived near Witney Mills. Marriott, his eldest son was my greatest friend all our school days. He had several sisters and younger brothers. Our workshops at the old home and the farmyard were great places for us to play hide and seek, and other games in the shops when wet, so that during the holidays we had good times together. Then we cut and rolled a cricket ground in the close and played cricket very much. There were no bathing places or baths, but we went to bathe all through the summer, bigger boys in the River Windrush and smaller in a back stream. One would imagine for small boys, who could not swim at first, bathing in the river of uneven depth would be dangerous, but I cannot call to mind any accident happening to any of us from bathing.

The winters seemed to have been much more severe in my boyhood, say 1868 to 1874 for we had skating every year, sometimes plenty of floods for miles. But at other times we had to walk two miles or more to a 'Ballast hole' by the railway and later to a large lake at Lynsham Hall.

It was not until later that we first saw a bicycle, all wood with about equal wheels and iron tyres, about 1875. I went to Abingdon in 1877 and then learned on the 'Boneshaker' as they were called. Boys had a great advantage in many ways when the bicycles with rubber tyres became to be used, but then we had not the smooth roads of the present days.

In the Autumn when cricket was over boys spent much of their time playing Marbles. I have not seen anyone playing for years, but they may do so in the villages. Every boy had his bag of marbles - several boys would play together, each putting up one to make a row of them. Then they lobbed at them from a measured distance, each keeping the ones he knocked off. Also a game called ring Taw. Marbles were placed round a ring marked out and from a distance a boy would have to shoot at them, holding the marble and shooting it with the thumb bent. This was a more advanced game.

Bowling hoops, too, was much practised, with an iron hoop of fairly good size - either by hitting with a stick or running them with a wire hook. Then of course hockey - the stick cut out of the hedgerow, or faggots. A straight stick with a good foot but at right angles, driving a bung.

Then where there was a farm yard boys played on the straw ricks and watched the men at work killing the mice in the corn ricks when being thrashed with a thrashing machine and engine. Some of the thrashing was done by two men in a barn, on the

thick oak floor, beating the corn out with 'flails' which required a good deal of practice, otherwise the loose bar of the flail had a tendency to give one a crack on the nut.

Boys always looked out for the pig killing - a pig was held by cords on a stool by two or three men and the butcher cut the throat. When bled it was laid flat on the ground, and others killed and laid side by side. They were then covered by a large heap of wheat straw which was set on fire, the butcher regulating it with a long handle prong and throwing off when the hair was burnt. They were then turned over and done the same way on the other side - afterwards scraped clean and the body cut open and the innards taken out. Then hung in the barn from hooks on strong chains to cool and get stiff. The pig was hung by the big hook going through the jaw. Even very heavy large pigs usually from ten to fifteen score as bacon pigs - big old ones as much as twenty five score or more. Porkers were small pigs which were scalded to get off the hair and scraped. In the South of England most of the pigs were done this way, and there they were hung up by the hind legs - smaller and not being made into bacon. Some bacon pigs were killed for the house and cut up, using some joints fresh and curing the sides and hams. We used to have half a dozen sides of bacon hung from the kitchen ceiling, cured in the winter to eat through the summer and autumn. Hams were pickled and hung longer but none of it was smoked.

Then there was the Cray fishing. The Windrush was good in parts for trout fishing with the fly. My brother Sam used to fish a good deal with a rod and line. The cray fishing was done as it was getting dark at night, and only in certain parts of the river. We had a meadow with a long piece of water where we went at the right season for them - Barley Harvest. Many would not know how they are caught so I will describe it. Small iron hoops about 18 inches in diameter are covered with a string netting which we used to make ourselves, beginning all round the hoop and finishing with a drop in the middle where the bait was tied on, herring or liver usually - three strings on the hoop joined together and then three or four yards long with a peg at the end. Taking about twenty of these nets you begin at one end of the water to lay them in likely places to catch the fish. With a long pole with a fork at the end, holding the string, it is lowered into the river near the bank where it is not too deep to lay flat on the bottom. By the time they are all placed it is time to draw up the first that were put in. Some nets when lifted out quickly will not have any on - then three or four with sometimes a dozen. We boys used to have to pick them off the nets as quickly as possible otherwise they got lost in the grass, being dark brown, then you have to pick them up by the back or they will pinch your finger with their claws. When they ran well we would get a bucket full, but say 100 - 200 did quite well. It was sometimes dark before we got home - we generally took bread and cheese and beer. They are afterwards treated like crabs, put into a large pot of boiling water making them a pink colour. Set round a dish they look very attractive and a delicacy in that part for tea.

Sparrow catching with long nets at night in the ivy, and bird trapping in various ways - picking them and then roasting them for supper. Tree climbing was much favoured in hot weather. We had a large clump of suitable trees from which we could climb from one to another. It was in the middle of the first close where the cricket ground is of late.

Then father employed an old carpenter who worked in a shed at the farm, mending and making implements and I remember a new wagon which single-handed took him a long time. The wood was all cut out from the tree timber at the saw pit, and the elm boards for the body of carts and wagons. I used to watch him at work when a small boy and as I grew up, lent him a hand occasionally. He was in regular employ but had a habit of drinking too freely at times when he would be away for weeks. Then was my opportunity of trying my hand, using the tools and mending things requiring it about the farm. We also did the painting too and I painted the name on the wagons and carts, then I was about 16 or 17 years old, by which time I was grown up strong and could carry sacks of corn or do the harvest work, loading wagons of corn or building the ricks.

Then in spring there was the bark harvest. In those days oak trees were cut down and barked by men in the woods and forests. The bark was propped up off the ground and allowed to dry, then brought in on wagons, stacked up high. My father was the only Bark merchant about the Witney district, and brought hundreds of tons which was cleaned and chopped up and sent in bags to the tanneries in London and Walsall.

It was either built up in large ricks or one or two barns were filled with it. Then we had two men who were occupied nearly all the year chopping the bark with a large flat chopper, on a high block, into small pieces. There were two women to each man, sitting on stools scraping all the moss and rough off the bark before it was cut. It was amusing as a boy to sit and watch these old women at work, chattering to one another. They seemed quite happy and when they left work to go home filled their aprons with the choppings and bits of wood to take home for their fires. The Tanners seal a bundle of bags, 100 at a time to be filled with bark, which was done by hanging them up from a beam in the barn, a hoop to keep the bag open, and then filled by one man with large wooden shovels whilst the other stood on a stool and rammed it down with a rammer. Then a woman sewed them up with string. It used to be my business to see to the weighing of the bark before it was taken by the railway van.

I now propose to record any remarkable coincidences and amusing incidents I can call to mind.

For instance, when I went up to the Head Office of the London and County Bank to see the Directors in 1877, who should come into the Chief Accountant's Office where I was, but my old playfellow Percy Clinch, then at Chubbs in London. I once or twice tried to arrange a meeting - but it never came off.

On an occasion when I went to London for bullion, from Petersfield, sitting in a restaurant, my brother Leonard came and sat down at the next table. When I went to the White City I think it was, who should I meet directly I got inside, but Leonard's wife Pat. When staying away at Hotels, it so frequently has happened that someone is acquainted with a mutual friend - the uncommon name of Shuffrey making it more conspicuous.

One day we had been on the bus to Boars Hill and I had been showing a friend my sketch. An old American gentleman heard my name and rushed up to me when we got down. 'Happy to meet you Mr Shuffrey, I have two of your pictures hanging in my home in America'. Where and when he got them I did not know!

I have been recognised as a Huguenot on two occasions, right away from Oxford, by perfect strangers who did not know my name. When going to a tobacconist shop at Canterbury, kept by an old gentleman, he wanted to know my name as he could see I was of Huguenot descent. Another occasion in 1922, after going to Scotland, we stayed at Alnwick on our return, and having some difficulty to get accommodation we went to the Old White Swan Hotel - getting there about lunchtime. We sat at small tables. After we had finished, an old gentleman who had been sitting at the next table with some ladies, came to me in the Hall – 'May I have a word with you - I can see you are a Huguenot'. I asked him why he should think so – 'Oh, I have been about the world'. He was formerly a sea captain. He seemed very delighted to make my acquaintance and when I came in after sketching wished to see my work. He introduced me to a friend of his who was a Town Councillor at Manchester, formerly a native of Alnwick. He bought my watercolour of the Castle and also asked me to do two others for him, which being fine I was able to do - altogether about £10, and I was only there from Saturday until Tuesday morning - some advantage in looking like a Huguenot.

Sketching is at times quite dangerous. When painting a view of Summerfield School, I was sitting for shade under the large elms in the playing fields. A number of boys were looking on, being their playtime. Only a few minutes after they had gone in I heard a crack, then another crack. Realising there was something wrong, without looking up I picked up my board from my knee and rushed out into the open - immediately a tremendous branch as thick as one's body came down just where I had been sitting. Had it been ten minutes earlier several deaths might have occurred. It was a fine summer morning and no wind - the foliage becomes heavy possibly.

On another occasion when sitting in the second quad at New College I was near the wall, where one would not expect anyone to come. Whilst sitting there painting, a gentleman came along and walked right into me, knocking me over and my paints all over the place, he being very startled. It turned out that he was blind and followed along the wall - rather a shock but no great harm to either.

People are generally friendly inclined to the Artist sketching, especially in the villages. When I was sketching the Notre Dame at Malines, Belgium, a Mr. Dieudonne came and asked me to his house when I had done. My wife was with me and we went to see them. He had a daughter who had been living in England who spoke English. They entertained us with cigars and beer. When the war began three years after, his daughter, who was then married, came to live with one of our friends in Oxford as a refugee, and came to see us. When war began people in the villages became very suspicious, thinking I was a German Spy. A curious thing happened. We were staying with our friends Mr & Mrs Tomes at Quainton and one day Mr Tomes drove us over to Whitchurch and left me sketching there, to walk back when finished. We went into the village and had tea at an Inn. After looking round we walked back through Tring where a farmer with his dogs came out and asked us which way we were going. We had some conversation with him as he knew our friends at Quainton. We heard through them afterwards that he had been told by the Police to see who it was, and people were sent all round to try and find what had become of me, thinking I was a German.

When I paid a visit to Quainton two years after, I went back by train and stayed at Claydon to have tea with friends on the way - going on by a later train. In the compartment was a young man in Khaki. Having

Plate 109 (above). Passport of James Allen Shuffrey for travel in Belgium, dated 8th July 1911. Shuffrey made two European sketching tours, the first in 1911 to Belgium and Trier in Germany, the second in 1914 at the time of the outbreak of the First World War.

Plate 110 (overleaf). Quai de Rosaire, Bruges, 1911. The faintly slumping gaggle of old waterside buildings with their decorative facades and spires are murkily reflected in the river. The bank forms a double curve leading the viewer into the picture which is terminated symmetrically by a single central bollard. Watercolour 355 x 279mm. Private collection.

Plate 111 (overleaf). Bacharach, 1914. The picture was left unfinished, and so is instructive in illustrating the order of work, as well as demonstrating that Shuffrey produced full-colour pictures on site at times. The artist carefully built up the central mass of colour, balancing cool (left) and warm (right) tones. The greater detail of the foreground, with the cottage garden wall re-using what appear to be grave slabs perhaps from the church whose lych-gate is seen to the right, contrasts with the impressionistic treatment of the ruinous castle beyond. The edges of the picture were left for last – in this case never finished, owing to the outbreak of World War I. Watercolour 330 x 418mm. Private collection.

Plate 112 (overleaf). Shuffrey's wartime sketching permit, two views dated 8th July 1918.

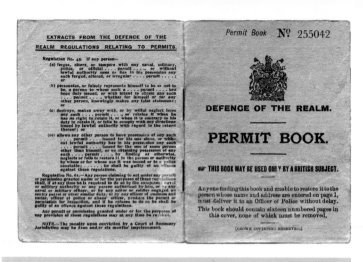

Plate 110

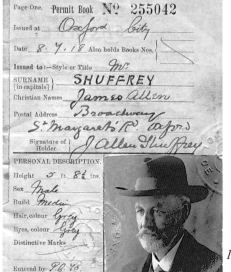

Plate 112

Plate 111

some conversation I found he came from Tring, having been home to help in the Harvest. Then he told me that soon after war began there was someone sketching at Whitchurch and when he went into the pub a policeman told him to ride round to see if he could find the man as he might be a German Spy - he said he was out till midnight. I told him I thought I knew who it was and he was much interested to find that I was the artist and as I happened to have the actual picture in my bag, got him to sign his name on the back of it. Extraordinary coincidence that I should have met him and got into conversation, there being no one else in the carriage. After a time anyone wishing to do any sketching had to get a permit, with a photograph inside and all particulars, from the Chief of Police, signed by a magistrate, and then apply to the Officer in charge of the district for permission. When sketching this was examined by Police - or if near the sea, by the Coastguard. Mr Tyrwhitt, our President of the Oxford Art society, brother of Admiral Tyrwhitt, was sketching in Edinburgh and the police took him to the Guard Room where he had to wait for some hours to verify his personality, and they confiscated the sketches he had been doing.

My wife was sitting by herself at Selsey making a very small sketch when the Coast Guard came along, stopped her and tore up her sketch. I have preserved our permit books as curiosities.

During the war I was too old for any service. My time was mostly spent in gardening and housework as my wife was out most days helping at the place where the soldiers' clothes were mended. Our domestic was required to help her father on his farm so that I got up to light the fire and get the breakfast for years. Potatoes and vegetables became so scarce that we had to eat rice instead and swedes if we could

get them. I therefore took an allotment on Port Meadow ground and grew all our potatoes, brussels sprouts etc., and also helped to plant some of our friends gardens, and grew as many tomatoes as possible. Everything became very dear. For some weeks we could not get a joint of meat and made use of ox tails for gravy. When ration cards came in the allowance of butter and sugar was very small. I did without butter and the others the sugar. Then there was the darkening of windows with blinds or curtains so that no light showed at night and no street lamps. Even large towns and cities were all in darkness under penalties. The Church and college clocks, including Big Tom at Christ Church did not strike so that the Zeppelins should not see the position of the towns from the air. In Oxford we had several warnings of raids but there was nothing more.

It was very amusing to see old gentlemen, and college dons, also ladies cultivating allotments and work was in full swing on Sundays. A large part of Port Meadow became allotments and Merton Fields was cultivated by the Varsity. I especially was amused to see an old Professor digging up a piece of grass. He had a line for each spit across and his daughter measured and marked out the width of each spit for him to dig. I had planted some onions, carrots etc. for a lady friend and they came up well and she thought how splendid the carrots were, of course 'heaps' too thick, so I began thinning them. Having done several rows my friend came back and saw what I had done and she got in quite a rage with me for spoiling her crop of carrots.

Another extraordinary coincidence occurred when I was living in the Old Farmhouse at Woodgreen in 1898. My nephew Leonard Junior was getting married and wanted the house which belonged to his father, so we had to hunt for a house and it ended in my buying 'The Laurels' at Bampton. We could not get in soon enough and we had a house lent us by a schoolmaster, Mr Thursfield. Now this was the house where Mr Charles Clinch lived when I was a boy, with a beautiful garden where I broke my leg. Curiously, whilst we were there Mrs Clinch and her son called at the house to know if they might walk round the old place. Imagine their surprise at finding me living in it as I had neither seen or heard of them for more than twenty years. Also my old friend Marriott Clinch came too. I had not seen him since he went to Portugal twenty years before and I did not see him again (or hear from him) until about 1928 - thirty years after when he got into the Burford bus and sat down next to me. I did not then know him but he recognised me and we travelled to Oxford together and he came and had tea with us. He had then retired and was looking for a house but got influenza and died.

Another remarkable incident of the kind occurred a few years ago. When we had been spending a fortnight or more in King's Lynn and Hunstanton we intended returning home, but before doing so I had a great desire to visit Blakeney and Cley, as Reg had been quartered there in the early days of the war. When sketching in Oxford a gentleman who was interested in my work suggested I should go to Norfolk and especially mentioned the George hotel, Blakeney. I therefore wrote to see if we could have accommodation for a few days and also to Wells on Sea and other hotels, but heard nothing suitable.

We were then returning home when a letter came from the George at Cley (my letter being sent on to them) offering rooms and also to meet us at Wells station, then the nearest. Buses did not then run. We decided at once to go and arrived at Cley the same evening. We found it very comfortable and were able to prolong our visit for a week. When returning from sketching at Blakeney we were walking along beside a stream where a gentleman was fishing and we got into conversation - mentioning Oxford and my name. He said at once 'my wife knows you and has a number of your postcards. My name is Bolton Smart and Mrs Smart is across the field sketching - I will call her'. Curiously - although the name did not convey anything to me I seemed to know who she was and remembered her well visiting Oxford with her father about twenty years before. Then it turned out that Col. Bolton Smart was a master at Charterhouse School and some boys in his house had been pupils of mine at Summerfield. We renewed our acquaintance as they were staying at Cley near our hotel.

When I bought the house in St Margaret's Road, really No. 99 Kingston Road (it had been called 19a St Margaret's), I was much struck with the fact of its being also 99 as we were then living at 99 Woodstock Road. Also my wife had a house at Berkhamsted, No. 99, High Street. I then looked up various numbers and dates. The house made the 19th house in our possession, and my 9th house to live in since I was married. I had bought the house on the 9th of March. Looking up other deeds of some cottages at Curbridge I had bought them on the 9th of May and sold them 19 years after, on the 9th of the month. As regards other events of my life, being born in 1859, I joined the London and County Bank at Oxford on April 9th, 1877 and retired 20 years after on April 9th.

Then many other matters seemed to occur on the 9th day or with 9 in it. For instance about that time I had exhibited as usual at the Art Society Exhibition but was much annoyed at one of my best pictures not being hung, as they said for want of space. I

Plate 113. Brasenose College. Watercolour by JA Shuffrey, published as a postcard in 1904. Private collection.

Plate 114. Combe, Woodstock. A child's view of this small and remote village – an endless green on an endless late summer's afternoon. The style is impressionistic. Watercolour 304 x 240mm. Private collection.

went to the room then at the back of the Clarendon Hotel in Frewin Court to tell Mr Grimsley the Secretary I should resign membership. Before telling him he said 'I have just sold a picture of yours, Didcot Church, to Miss Hyde.' I said, what is the number, 99? To my surprise it was so numbered. Selling this picture caused me to alter my mind and continue my membership, being elected soon after on the Committee and also the Hanging Committee, and after some years in 1922, elected Hon. Secretary in place of Matthew Webb, then too ill. I was in Scotland at Callender when I received the notice to my surprise - so it is rather remarkable that selling picture No 99 altered the course of events in my connection with the Art Society and this year, 1931, nine years after, my work has had the best press notices and I was interviewed on my birthday by the Oxford Mail which gave me a column in their paper, on my Art life, congratulations on my birthday, 72, and portrait in the paper, (none of which would have occurred).

In the wartime I saw there was a sale at Miss Hodets, Park Road, and I found that particular picture of mine, No 99 was amongst other artists works for sale, Things then were almost given away. I waited intending to bid it up which was then knocked down to me at a £1. Requiring a picture at the time to send to the Old Dudley Exhibition in London I sent it priced £5.5s. and it was sold - so I was fortunate with it again.

Plate 115. Adderbury Church. Both the location north of Oxford near Banbury and the proportions of the picture are unusual for the artist. Watercolour 304 x 152mm. Private collection.

Plate 116. St Mary the Virgin, south porch. Watercolour. Private collection.

Plate 117. Magdalen College, south-west corner of Great Quad, Watercolour. Ashmolean Museum WA OA 376.

Plate 118. Photograph of the artist, probably taken in the 1920s. Shuffrey poses with a volume closely resembling Francis Nicholson's *Drawing and Painting from Landscape* of 1823, against a background of rugged landscape scenes relating to his annual painting tours.

James Allen Shuffrey: A Chronology

1713	House at the top of Narrow Hill, Woodgreen, Witney bought by Huguenot immigrant John Shuffrey. Weaving workshops erected at the back of the house.
1720	Marriage of John Shuffrey.
1859	James Allen Shuffrey born at Woodgreen, Witney, and christened at Holy Trinity Church.
1863	Attends local celebrations on the wedding day of the Prince of Wales.
1864-68	Attends Mrs Floyd's school, Narrow Hill, Woodgreen, Witney.
1868-73	Attends Mr Collier's school in the Corn Exchange, Witney, passing the Cambridge Local Examinations in six subjects in 1872.
1874-76	At home learning farming, gardening and poultry keeping.
1875	Death of Shuffrey's mother
1877-82	Clerk at Abingdon Branch of the London and County Bank, lodging with James Gibbens, harnessmaker. Takes up cycling, commences sketching, joins Rowing Club, joins Musical Association, joins choir of St Michael's Church, joins Abingdon Dramatic Society.
1878	Joins 1st Berkshire Volunteers, earns Certificate of St John's Ambulance Association, participates in the Great Volunteer Review of 1881 by Queen Victoria in Windsor Park.
1879	First sketching tour, of the south coast, based at Eastbourne.

1882-84	Moved to Arundel branch of London and County Bank. Continues sketching and begins to sell his watercolours. Joins church choir.
1886	Shuffrey's views of Arundel area exhibited, along with the work of other London and County Bank staff, at the Guildhall, London.
1884-96	Moved to Petersfield branch of London and County Bank, lodging initially in Sheep Street. Joins church choir and Musical Society. Becomes Honorary Secretary of the Church of England Temperance Society.
1885	Marriage to Esther Walker at Denchworth Church, Oxfordshire. Newly-weds move to Laureldean, Petersfield.
1886	Reginald born at Laureldean.
1887	Shuffrey designs a mug and cup for the Petersfield celebrations of the Queen's Golden Jubilee.
1887-93	Serves as Honorary Secretary of the Petersfield Horticultural Show; elected a Fellow of the Royal Horticultural Society. Acts as Vice-President of the Literary and Debating society.
1889	Death of Shuffrey's father Samuel.
1892	Barbara born.
1893	Family move to Heath Villa, Petersfield.
1896	Moved to Romford branch of London and County Bank, now as Cashier.
1897	Retires from bank owing to ill health. Family lives temporarily at Woodgreen, Witney. Becomes drawing master to pupils at Bampton vicarage.
1898-1902	Shuffrey and family live at The Laurels, Bampton. Becomes Secretary of the Bampton Horticultural Show. Holds successful exhibitions of his pictures at Bampton School and at the Corn Exchange, Witney.
1898,1900	Exhibits pictures at the Oxford Art Society exhibition, and is elected a member in 1900.
1902	Shuffrey and family move to Thorncliffe Road, Summertown, Oxford. Shuffrey paints college views for Ryman's Picture Dealers, High Street and for postcards, and teaches a drawing class.
1903	Visit to Arncliffe, Yorkshire.
1904	Designs postcard pictures for R Peel, Alden & Co and Faulkner & Co, London; also doing photography.
1905	Death of Esther Shuffrey.
1906	Shuffrey and children move to 51 Holywell Street, Oxford. Shuffrey showing pictures regularly at the Assembly Rooms, Town Hall, and the Arts and Crafts Exhibition. Shuffrey's first London show, at Dickinson and Forster in Bond Street.
1906-08	Shuffrey and Reginald take a studio behind the Clarendon Hotel in Cornmarket Street.
1907	The Great Oxford Pageant – Shuffrey, Reginald and Barbara take part.
1908	Marriage to Rose Lane, and honeymoon in the Lake District, the first of a long series of sketching tours.
1909	Sketching tour of Berkhamsted, Hemel Hempstead and area.

1910	Sketching tour of North Devon, Minehead to Clovelly.
1911	Sketching tour of Barmouth and Dolgelly; and of Belgium and Trèves.
1912	Sketching tours of Hastings, Tye and Winchelsea; Canterbury; Chester and Shrewsbury.
1912-30	Art teacher at Summerfields School, Summertown, Oxford.
1913	Sketching tours of Whitby and coast towns; and of Durham and Richmond.
1914	Sketching tour of the Rhine: Cologne, Coblenz, Remagen, Rhens, Boppard, Caub, Goarhausen, Oberwessel, Baccharach. Return via Amsterdam upon the outbreak of war.
1915	Sketching tour of Burnham, Glastonbury, Bristol, Wye Valley and Chepstow.
1916	Sketching tour of Hinton Parva, the Berkshire Downs and Quainton.
1917	Sketching tour of Chepstow, Bristol, the Wye Valley, Hereford and Ross.
1918	Sketching tour of Looe, Polperro and Fowey.
1919	Sketching tour of North Wales, Harlech, Criccieth, Bedgelert.
1920	Sketching tour of Tenby, Saundersfort, Lydsty Manor and Pembroke.
1921	Sketching tour of Seaton, Lyme Regis, Dorchester, Frome.
1922	Elected to the committee and made Honorary Secretary of the Oxford Art Society. Sketching tour of Edinburgh, Stirling, Callender and the Trossachs, Dunbar, Berwick, Alnwick.
1923	Sketching tour of St Ives, Falmouth, Totnes and Bath.
1924	Sketching tour of King's Lynn, Hunstanton, Blakeney and Cley, and Norwich.
1925	Sketching tour of Bury St Edmunds, Walbwerswick and Southwold.
1926	Sketching tours of Isle of Wight; and Burnham, Lynmouth and Ilfracombe.
1927	Sketching tour of Bournemouth, Salcombe and Mevagissy.
1928	Sketching tours of Ventnor, Isle of Wight; and of Gadshill, Hunstanton, Lincoln and Peterborough.
1929	Sketching tour of Saracens, Woking, Witley, Taunton, Wiviliscombe
1930	Anniversary Exhibition of the Oxford Art Society at the Randolph Hotel. Sketching tour of Saracens, Godalming and Charterhouse, Windsor and Eton.
1931	Sketching tour of Torquay, Totnes and Bath.
1932	Sketching tour of Sidmouth and Exeter.
1933	Sketching tour of Port Isaac and Padstow.
1934	Sketching tour of Worthing, Bramber.
1935	Gives collection of watercolour pictures and pencil drawings to Oxford. Sketching tour of Ludlow, Bridgnorth and Sidmouth.
1936	Sketching tour of Weymouth.
1939	Death of James Allen Shuffrey on 18th July.

Plate 119. *The Botanical Gardens, Oxford, 1917.* The south face of Magdalen College's Bell Tower warmly lit by the early autumn sunlight, was seen facing the tramcar in the picture *Plate 35.* Here it dominates the background. We are standing just inside the entrance to the Botanic Garden looking back at the entrance archway of the early 1630s by Nicholas Stone, with its charming mixture of classical and Renaissance elements. Watercolour. Private collection.

Bibliography

Baldry, AL 'William Turner of Oxford, Water-Colour Painter. Born 1789. Died 1862', in *Walker's Quarterly* No 11 (April 1923)

Bodleian Library, *Supplement to the Staff Calendar*, (Oxford, Horace Hart, 1907)

Buckler, JC *Drawings of Oxford. 1811-1827* (Bodleian Library, Oxford, 1951)

Byatt, Anthony, *Picture Postcards and their Publishers* (Golden Age Postcard Books, 1978)

Connor, Patrick *Michael Angelo Rooker 1746-1801* (Batsford, 1984)

Coyish, AW *The Dictionary of Picture Postcards in Britain 1894-1939* (Antique Collectors' Club, 1984)

Graham, Malcolm *Henry Taunt of Oxford. A Victorian Photographer* (The Oxford Illustrated Press, 1973)

Graham, Malcolm *Images of Victorian Oxford* (Sutton, 1992)

Harrison, Colin *John Malchair of Oxford* (Ashmolean Museum, Oxford, 1998)

Harrison, Colin *Turner's Oxford* (Ashmolean Museum, Oxford, 2000)

Nairn, Ian and Pevsner, Nikolaus *Sussex. The Buildings of England*, Penguin Books (Harmondsworth, 1965)

Nicholson, Francis *The Practice of Drawing and Painting from Landscape in Water Colours* (London, John Murray, 1820)

Perrot, John *Iffley Water Mill – A History* (Iffley Local History Society Publication No. 3, after 1996)

Petter, Helen Mary *The Oxford Almanacks* (Oxford, Clarendon Press, 1974)

Pevsner, Nikolaus *Berkshire. The Buildings of England*, Penguin Books (Harmondsworth, 1966)

Pevsner, Nikolaus and Sherwood, Jennifer *Oxfordshire. The Buildings of England*, Penguin Books (Harmondsworth, 1974)

Royal Commission on Historical Monuments, England. An inventory of Historical Monuments in the City of Oxford (RCHM, 1939)

Shuffrey, HJ *The Bodleian about 1863* (Bodleian Library manuscript)

Shuffrey, JA *Churches of Abingdon & neighbourhood, sketched by J Allen Shuffrey in the years 1877-8* (Bodleian Library manuscript MS D gen.c.9)

Shuffrey, JA 'Album': *J Allen Shuffrey* (Bodleian Library manuscript MS D gen.c.8)

Shuffrey, JA *Catalogue of an Exhibition of watercolours of English landscapes by J A Shuffrey* at Dickinson's Galleries, New Bond Street from September 20th to October 3rd 1906

Shuffrey, JA *Catalogue of an exhibition of Watercolours of Oxford Cathedral and Colleges, Blenheim, Surrey Commons and the Wye Valley* on view at his studio, Clarendon Yard, Cornmarket from 23 May to 13 July 1907

Shuffrey JA *Catalogue of an exhibition of watercolours and black & white of north Devon and Clovelly, the English Lakes, Oxford and the neighbourhood* at Ryman's Gallery, 23 High Street, Oxford, May 30 – June 13 (c 1912)

Shuffrey, J Allen *Rural Oxford*. Sketches of Picturesque and Interesting Places on the Motor Bus Routes in the County Districts around Oxford (City of Oxford Motor Services, 1934)

Shuffrey, Margaret and Tony *The Painting Tours of James Allen Shuffrey, from 1877 to 1936* (private publication, 1987)

Shuffrey, Margaret and Tony *The Shuffrey Family* (private publication, 1987)

The Victoria History of the Counties of England. *A History of Oxfordshire* Vol IV: *Oxford* (Oxford University Press, 1979)

The Victoria History of the Counties of England. *A History of Oxfordshire* Vol XIII: *Bampton Hundred* (1996)

Wilcox, Timothy and Titterington, Christopher *William Turner of Oxford (1780-1862)* (Oxfordshire County Museum Service, 1984)

Plate 120. A Cotswold House and Garden. This unsigned and undated watercolour picture of a charming late Victorian garden in West Oxfordshire is plainly by Shuffrey, and may relate to his time at Bampton in the 1890s. OXCMS:1999.53.